GROW OR DIE

GROW OR DIE

*Essays on Church Growth
to Mark the 900th Anniversary of
Winchester Cathedral*

———

edited by
Alexander Wedderspoon

LONDON · SPCK

First published 1981
SPCK
Holy Trinity Church
Marylebone Road
London NW1 4DU

Acknowledgements

The quotation from 'New Year Letter' by W. H. Auden is
reprinted from *Collected Poems* by permission of Faber and Faber.

The quotation from 'Church Going' by Philip Larkin is reprinted
from *The Less Deceived* by permission of The Marvell Press,
England.

Printed and bound in Great Britain at
The Camelot Press Ltd, Southampton

ISBN 0 281 03789 2

Cover: The illustration on the cover is *The Salvation*, one of a series
of sixteen Festival Banners, on the theme of the Old and the New
Creation, painted for the 900th anniversary of Winchester
Cathedral by Thetis Blacker. The Cross is seen as the Tree of
Life, a symbol of growth, with its roots in the world's sin, suffering
and death which are transformed by the radiant and glorious
Christ into the flowers and fruits of heaven.

Contents

Foreword

by

ROBERT RUNCIE

Archbishop of Canterbury

'The Church goes on. Its adversaries have demolished it a thousand times in argument and pronounced it a dead thing and cried to carry out the corpse for all was over bar the shouting; they have even taken themselves to shouting, only to find that when it was all over the slain Hydra had raised a new head and all had to be done again. For the Lord is risen, and the Easter hope inexhaustible.' These words of the historian J. N. Figgis might well form a text for *Grow or Die*.

You will find within the pages of this encouraging book evidence of a recovery of nerve, a renewal of trust; but there is also a sober realism.

We cannot behave as if the critical work of the past couple of decades had never happened. There is a danger that in some parts of the world people are finding it too easy to believe and to ignore the very important questions which have been raised in recent years. The cure for Christian confusion is not Christian dogmatism or over-confidence; but some of those who are attracted to the enthusiastic sects might be forgiven sometimes for thinking that the Church of England had lost touch with the joy and positive affirmations of the Christian gospel. Too often we have been immobilized by a sense of the complexity of things, and a cloud of conflicting witnesses has concealed things which have never been more obvious to eyes formed by the experience of Christ.

Fear and selfishness, the roots of dis-ease, can be overcome by the love of God and trust in Christ. The best way we can help the world now is not by being conformed to its own self-doubt and confusion but by humbly turning to explore and value our traditional faith and point to where it has seeds for growth.

There are two fresh insights which are not articulated in detail but which lie behind all that is said here about growth. The first is a recognition that no single form of Christian experience, conviction or organization is going to prevail over others. Conservative and radical, contemplative and activist, pietist and social reformer, all must learn to live together. They may and should see much to criticize in their own and each others' position. The critical faculty must not be lost. Reverence for truth must still be paramount. But all must learn to live together, for in religion, as in all else, the same things do not appeal to everybody. The second insight is that nothing lasts as long as it used to. The life expectations of so many of our customs, ideas and institutions are bound to be dramatically shortened. Is it really to be expected in such times as these that the Church should come up straight away with all the right answers? It is possible to pretend to have them, but all too easy to see through the pretence.

In a period of profound transformation, exploration must precede discovery. But exploration involves risk. The Church cannot be expected to learn from its mistakes unless it is bold enough to make some. So working hypotheses replace settled systems, short-term projects are substituted for permanent organization – and it is right that our churches should be furnished with stackable chairs rather than immovable pews.

The faith without which there would be no true growth, must be the faith of Abraham, of Jesus, and of the Church which confesses a crucified and risen Lord. It is faith in a God who is not hemmed in by the enterprises which are undertaken in his name, who is neither caught out by their failure nor satisfied by their success. Our enterprises today must be seen to be far more provisional than were those of our Victorian or medieval predecessors; but they must be fuelled by the unchanging Easter faith.

The stories told in the following pages are of more than merely ecclesiastical interest and importance. Bishop Leslie Hunter has told a contemporary legend:

> As the threats of war and the cries of the dispossessed were sounding in his ears, Western man fell into an uneasy sleep. In his sleep he dreamed that he entered a spacious store in which the gifts of God to men are kept, and addressed the angel behind the counter, saying, 'I have run out of the fruits of the Spirit, can you restock me?' When the angel seemed about to say no, he burst out, 'In place of war, afflictions, injustice, lying and lust, I need love, joy, peace, integrity, discipline. Without these I shall be lost.' And the angel behind the counter replied, 'We do not stock fruits, only seeds.'

Despite its title, this is not a book nervously obsessed by the need for survival. It might even have been called 'Die and Grow'.

ROBERT CANTUAR:

Easter 1981

Introduction

The Church of England has been in steady decline for decades and in steep decline since the mid-1960s. Look at some of the facts and figures:

1. Despite an increase in the population, the number of ordained clergymen in the Church of England has declined from over 24,000 at the start of this century to just over 11,000 at present – of which number a substantial percentage are members of the Non-Stipendiary Ministry and so not engaged in full time pastoral work.[1]

2. In the fifteen years between 1963 and 1978 the number of men ordained each year declined from over 650 to 350, despite official protestations that a minimum of 500 new men were required each year merely to maintain the status quo.[2]

3. In the same fifteen-year period the number of persons confirmed into church membership each year declined from 190,000 to 100,000 [3]

4. In 1964, 46% of all marriages took place in parish churches of the Church of England and 30% in civil ceremonies in Register Offices. Ten years later the figures were reversed: 34% of marriages took place in Church and 47% in Register Offices.[4]

5. A realistic estimate would be that about $2\frac{1}{2}$ to 3% of the total adult population attend the parish churches of the Church of England on an average Sunday and that this number increases to about 5%[5] at the major festivals of Christmas and Easter. These figures correspond to the findings of the Report 'Prospects for

the Eighties', published in 1980 and based on a census of the
churches undertaken in 1979 by the Nationwide Initiative in
Evangelism.

The decline of the Church has produced a considerable literature
of analysis and self-criticism.

In his book *The Church of England in Crisis*, published in 1973,
Canon Trevor Beeson wrote: 'The low morale of the Church of
England is directly related to the falling away of support which has
characterised the whole of the twentieth century and has become
even more marked during the past decade.'[6]

Writing as a Free Churchman, Dr Daniel Jenkins commented in
1975 that, 'The Church of England gives the impression that she
has lost heart . . . and that she is resigning herself to conducting a
retreat, characteristically slow and cautious, into denominational
status. . . . Ours are old and tired churches, set within old and tired
nations.'[7]

In 1977, John Bowden, the Managing Director of the SCM
Press, painted a picture of almost unrelieved gloom and failure:
'The Churches are dying and statistics are there to confirm what
first-hand impressions convey . . . expectations of growth, or even
much change is minimal.'[8] 1979 saw the publication of *The Fate of
the Anglican Clergy* by two sociologists, Robert Towler and
A. P. M. Coxon. They argued that the full-time parish clergy of
the Church of England can now be regarded as an endangered
species, to be rendered extinct sooner rather than later on account
of their social irrelevance and lack of professional credibility.

Whatever else the Church may have lacked in recent years, it
has not lacked prophets of gloom.

1979 saw the 900th Anniversary celebrations of Winchester
Cathedral. The event was marked by a wide range of activities: the
Bishop and the Dean accompanied the cathedral choir on a much
appreciated tour of North America; there was an extensive programme of special services, concerts and lectures; the cathedral and
its activities featured on TV and radio in Britain and elsewhere in
the world; there were more than 500,000 visitors. Such

celebrations are valuable and important for their own sake, but the Dean and Chapter also felt the need to mark the anniversary by some rather more permanent contribution to the life and thought of the Church.

Perhaps our judgement was influenced by the euphoria of our celebrations, but it seemed to us that the prophets of gloom were looking at the Church through eyes which were excessively blinkered and bleary. It seemed to us more than high time that the Church began to learn from its achievements rather than its failures, to affirm its faith rather than to advertise its doubts. Suppose that, instead of emphasizing the negative and stressing the Church's failings and follies, we were to do the very opposite?

So it was that we invited the Bishops of Winchester and Wakefield, the Dean of St Paul's, and a recent Moderator of the General Assembly of the Church of Scotland to write on the question: 'As you go about your daily work and ministry and as you reflect on the Church as you experience it, where do you see signs of encouragement, growth and hope?' We invited the distinguished theologian and churchman, Dr F. W. Dillistone, to write on the question: 'As you look back on the Church as it was fifty years ago and as you reflect on it today, what gives you most reason for encouragement?' We invited the General Secretary of one of the Church's leading missionary societies to write on the question: 'As you travel throughout the churches of the world-wide Anglican Communion do you find them everywhere in decline? Where do you see the signs of renewal and of growth?' Their replies form much of the substance of this book.

Sheer limitation of space demands that this publication is mainly concerned with the problems of the Church of England. As the established church it has a pastoral concern for all who call themselves 'C. of E.', whether they are active church members or not. This presents particular difficulties and opportunities and in this respect the Church of England corresponds more closely to the Church of Scotland than to any of the other denominations in England. Besides, to attempt a publication of this kind on a fully ecumenical basis would be to risk ending up with a volume so vast that few would wish to read it – and fewer still be able to buy it. But this limitation should not be taken as implying any lack of ecumenical concern – as the contents will make clear.

The title 'Grow or Die' is addressed to the Church as a whole and it should not be taken as implying a retreat into blind in-flexibility, e.g. the idea that every individual church building must always be kept open as a church, come what may. It is no more than commonsense that a church building may need to be closed if, for example, the local population has moved away in the course of urban development. Likewise the term 'Growth' includes not only growth in numbers but growth in Christian influence in society, growth in Christian service and growth in Christian prayer and spirituality.

No one would pretend that this publication represents any kind of 'blue-print for renewal' – the Church of England does not take kindly to such documents. It is a subjective and impressionistic survey by busy men. It will provide ideas, stimulate comparisons and provoke controversies. It deserves study, thought and discussion by clergy and lay persons throughout the country. If it serves to create a more positive mood throughout the Church it will have amply fulfilled its purpose.

NOTES

1. *Sheffield Report*. General Synod of C. of E. 1974
2. Statistical Supplement to *C. of E. Year Book, 1980*. C.I.O.
3. Ibid.
4. *Marriage and the Church's Task* (C.I.O. 1978), p. 114.
5. For this figure see Argyle and Beit Hallahmi, *The Social Psychology of Religion* (Routledge & Kegan Paul 1975), p. 9.
6. Davis Poynter 1973, p. 40.
7. *The British, their Identity and their Religion* (SCM 1975), p. 68.
8. *Voices in the Wilderness* (SCM 1977), p. 3.

ONE

Signs of Growth in the Church of England
New shoots from an old tree

The Right Reverend JOHN V. TAYLOR,
Bishop of Winchester

For what it is worth the charts are showing an up-turn. The Statistical Unit of the Church of England states that, compared with the year 1976, the number of baptisms increased by 7·7%, all Sunday communicants by 8·1%, and Christmas communicants by 10·5%. General Sunday attendance at church services was up by 0·5%. The year 1978 produced the highest number of confirmation candidates since 1973. The number of men offering as candidates for ordination in 1978 was 13·6% higher than in 1974; those recommended for training were 10·6% more. Looking beyond the narrow statistics of church attendance, the audience capacity for religious programmes on TV and radio is quite significant. The religious music programme on Radio Solent, *Ancient and Modern*, boasts around 45,000 listeners, which puts it among the most popular in the business, a little ahead of the secular request programmes and far beyond the number listening to Saturday afternoon sports.

The changes are only slight, especially when one remembers the steady increase of population, and we have no guarantee that they will persist. Yet they have solid value precisely because they are the overall figures. They do not reflect merely the dramatic upsurge of a few exceptional congregations, which is usually accomplished at the expense of neighbouring churches; they show the Church as a whole actually gaining a little ground, and this has far more significance than the addition of a few thousand new adherents; it proves that the downward trend does not *have* to go on. It gives the lie to the statistical prophets of doom. I, for one, do not believe that the things which statistics can prove are the most significant, but the fog of gloom which they have generated can now at least be lifted, and this may give us a better chance of seeing all those more important indications of growth and vitality that we have been too despondent to notice before.

Before we try to identify some of these signs of growth, I think it will be helpful to try to understand a little better the real cause of our recent despondency. For the statistics alone cannot account for it; elsewhere in the world Christians who are fewer than 1% of the population bear a confident and joyful witness, and in the West the Church has known periods of worse recession without losing its nerve. We have been unmanned not by numbers but by change. The twentieth century has brought upon us one of those mutations of corporate consciousness, of which perhaps the last example was the Renaissance. It is not simply a change of fashion nor the normal *avant garde* of a new generation, nor can we dismiss it as the 'spirit of the age' on which the Church is warned not to model herself. It is a shift of emphasis, of balance, of direction, which is happening, here a little and there a little, like eddies on the surface of the sea which at first seem unrelated, but cumulatively show that the tide has turned.

There is a universal shift from passivity under some hierarchy of authority towards expectations of collaboration and co-responsibility. People are no longer asking about routine (how is it always done?) but about purpose (what is the best way of achieving our aim?). The old juridical mentality (what is legally permitted?) is rapidly giving place to personal responsiveness (what is humanly required?). Policies dictated from above are rejected in favour of *ad hoc* decisions based on shared experience. People are less and less able to learn from instruction and precept and find they can more readily learn through questioning and experience, and so educational method is being remodelled accordingly. There is less reliance on ideas logically argued and more on feeling and non-verbal communication.

All these trends are evident in every westernized society today anywhere in the world. Naturally there is a backlash of traditionalism and authoritarianism, but the preference for responsible participation, and the reliance on experience rather than precept, spread like a steady tide in the affairs of men. I believe that when the Church is able to respond to this deep current of change in the consciousness of mankind then the supernatural factor in her life will again appear as something relevant and available to the life of the world. But in the meantime this change has caused our heavily institutionalized Church to suffer a loss of direction, deep shock and subsequent depression, and one symptom of this has been an angry and irrational *death wish* evident in a rigidity in the selection and training of persons for the ministry, consequent unnecessary amalgamations of parishes, and a sterile stonewalling in ecumenical relations. The situation is actually rich with positive promise, but if we want to grasp the opportunities we must stop exaggerating the negatives.

I could easily fill the rest of this chapter with examples of traditional parishes that have 'come alive' to an extraordinary degree and are growing rapidly both in numbers and in quality of life. In their various ways they show that, *given similar circumstances,* what has worked in the past can still work today. The congregation of St Michael-le-Belfry in York, under the inspired preaching ministry of David Watson, shows that an All Souls', Langham Place, can be transported to the North with a more adventurous and updated use of drama and dance and general freedom in worship. Ashtead, Surrey, is one random instance among many that might be given of highly successful church growth in a fairly well-to-do suburban parish, with a recently renewed electoral roll of 1,200 in a population of about 14,000, and 400-500 children in various teaching groups leading to an annual 'output' of some sixty confirmation candidates each year. In both these examples, incidentally, a convinced policy of establishing house-groups has been an important feature, supplementing the more traditional approach to the parochial ministry; but my purpose in quoting them is to demonstrate that there is no reason why a traditional pattern of ministry in one of the traditional styles of community should not produce the same level of church growth as it has in the past.

But that, of course, begs several questions. How much of the 'church growth' in one parish consists of refugees from dying churches round about? In any case, must we not in these days look for a less restricted level of expansion than the normal life of a congregation provides for? For it has been demonstrated beyond question, even at St Michael-le-Belfry in York, that, once the numbers of a congregation have reached a certain ceiling, no amount of effort will give any permanent increase. As quickly as new members are brought in others will leave, because 'the crowd' has become too large to provide what people are seeking in a congregation. The congregation, as such, is no longer a context for further growth, so a different context needs to be found, either in subsidiary congregations or in a steady proliferation of house-groups.

But the most serious question that has to be faced by those who base their optimism on successful examples of *traditional* parochial ministry is this: What happens when the traditional style of community for which that ministry was devised has disappeared? That traditional ministry never did break through the major frontier in our society to catch the imagination and the allegiance of the working class. Anyone who is serious about evangelism and church growth must look to those who are trying to forge new forms of church life on council estates, in the places where men and women actually spend their working hours, in the deprived centres of our cities and in our main multi-racial communities. It is when we look in these directions that we see the small beginnings of the most authentic new growth in the Christian presence in England today.

I start with the council estates – the homes of what is probably the largest section of the English population. Several of the best agencies of social research and consultation which are serving the Church today have concentrated on this field, there is a large literature and the theological colleges are spending a great deal of time on this aspect of training for the Ministry. To generalize would make dull reading, and in any case no two situations are identical, so I can best indicate the liveliness of these new developments by quoting from the self-assessment written by one Anglican priest as part of an in-service training project. He

describes with great thoroughness the life-pattern of a huge new
overspill town of ex-Londoners. He knows the wage structure of
his people and the different work they do, the sources of their discontent and the pattern of their ambitions. It is a totally planned
place; there has been nothing organic or gradual in its growth. It is
not a place in which anyone wants to put down roots and grow
old. There is a great deal of friendliness and helpfulness but no
community and very little willingness on anyone's part to take a
lead.

The element of growth in this man's ministry and that of a great
many others like him is not to be found in anything that he does
nor in any new technique but in the openness of his mind. He is a
discoverer searching all the time for a truer theological understanding of the shape and nature of the situation in which he and his
neighbours live their lives, and learning this from them and with
them.

I read quite a lot of theology and have two main interests. One is the
Bible, which I find increasingly fascinating and part of me wishes I
could go off and spend a lot more time studying it. My other
theological interest is the reading of 'secular literature' and seeing how
it relates to theology.

I suppose I can sum up my central theological idea in a sentence of
Bonhoeffer: 'The Church is Jesus Christ experienced in community.' I
have seen my job in terms of helping to build up a sense of identity and
unity in the whole place, especially among the congregation. We have
no church building, so we use the Roman Catholic school hall. I came
to see that the vision we needed was the vision of the people of Israel in
the desert, carrying God around with them in a tent, as it were. Much
of my time, energy and preaching has been spent in emphasising the
fact that the Christian life is not detached or semi-detached, but a
common life. Sunday lunch together as a Church two or three times a
year with about sixty people, a parish camp in the New Forest to
which about thirty people have come and had a week's holiday
together, day trips to the seaside. At the Eucharist we take a long time
about the Peace and everybody goes on a walkabout greeting
everyone else without necessarily shaking hands. Each year our plan is
to have three six-week terms in which we meet once a week for a
course of study or discussion. Two prayer groups meet weekly. My

basic premise about worship is that it must offer to God the life of the place in which it is being offered, and that people sharing in it for the first time must recognise it as such, even though they may not understand what the Eucharist is. Each Sunday we have between 40 and 50 communicants, and over a period of a month about 90 different people receive Communion. They do a wide range of jobs. Half a dozen men work in one capacity or other in the local factory estate, most of them on the shop floor. There is a doctor and his wife from the hospital, an ambulance driver, a couple of policemen, a social worker, a teacher at the local comprehensive school and his wife, an aircraft engineer, a glass salesman, a gas service engineer. Nearly all the women who come are housewives with small children. Many of the people who come to church here left school without any exam. qualifications at all. To see them grow in confidence when they have taken on a Sunday lunch for about 60 people and made a great success of it has been a joy for me, for it has always been undertaken with a great sense of foreboding and dread. Decisions are taken at the Church Committee which consists of 10 people and is a very easy, relaxed group.

I live in a house identical with all the others around and I make sure that it is indistinguishable, with no signs saying Vicarage or any aggressive ecclesiastical ornament. It also helps that I have a neurotic dog and three small sons who are saints only in name. I do not see myself as part of the local élite, and deliberately discourage others from seeking me as part of it either. I have refused to stand as a school manager, but have encouraged members of the congregation to do so. I spend a lot of my time doing general visiting, which includes pre-baptism visiting. Some people come and ask for prayers or a visit. Going shopping at the estate supermarket just up the road can become a major pastoral exercise. I spend a couple of hours each week in term time in the schools. I spend some time too with the people that I call 'hinges' in the place – school caretakers, District Nurses, etc. Two members of the congregation run a club for children between the age of 7 and 14 which fulfils a great need. They are self-financing but see what they are doing as very much part of the work of the Church. The nun who works with me runs a 'no strings attached' coffee morning in the community wing of the comprehensive school. We do a house-to-house collection for Christian Aid on the largest of these estates. We also put a Christmas card through every door.

What does it amount to – 200 adults perhaps, committed in some degree to a Christian fellowship that is aware of itself as a community but almost lost from sight in a population of 13,000? It is evidence of new life precisely because they are together feeling their way and are not merely reiterating assumptions from another time and another place. It is a genuinely indigenous Church, experimenting in its own mission. The priest himself is ever ready to re-examine his own hypothesis.

> What is the theology of a place like this? Which part of the Christian tradition is the one which speaks most directly to our condition? Having no church building in this place helps people to see it as little more than a transit camp. I now see that my particular emphasis on Abraham and living in tents carries all this one stage further. I need to think hard about the significance of a church building from a 'folk religion' point of view. Would it help them even if the majority never came to it? Perhaps another way of looking at the theology is to emphasise the *newness* of the life here and see that as something positive. There is after all a lot in the Gospel about newness, though it is not easy to see these estates as the New Jerusalem!

In many of the deprived and almost derelict centres of our great cities the Church is beginning to show the same courageous readiness to re-think. Clergy and committed lay people together are taking the trouble to 'do their homework', starting *de novo* to understand the basic sociological facts of the situation there, and asking themselves 'which part of the Christian tradition is the one which speaks most directly' to their condition. The residents of the city centre today are there for the most part because they are the most vulnerable and powerless members of society and least able to obtain more desirable housing within reach of a job. In one way or another they need a champion, a spokesman. The witnesses of Jesus Christ in such a situation are bound to adopt some aspects of liberation theology. Willy-nilly they are involved in social issues and find themselves taking up causes, whether it be housing or play space, school standards or public transport, job-creation or resistance to racism. Old fashioned Anglo-Catholics and Conservative Evangelicals alike have learned to see this development as the face which the gospel must necessarily wear when it is truly proclaimed to the poor. This in itself is a most significant sign of new growth.

A striking new feature in these areas of mission is the sacrificial readiness of young Christian couples to move into the down-town streets and make their homes there in order to participate more fully in the witness of that church with which they have chosen to identify themselves. It is, in fact, becoming more common, in places other than the inner city, for committed Christians to choose their place of residence with an eye on the particular church with which they wish to become involved. This, of course, reflects a middle-class mobility and freedom of choice, and it could lead to the creation merely of more eclectic congregations, saying the correct things about mission but creating a selfconsciously alien group rather than an indigenous Church. So far, however, the number of people taking this step remains small and one must honour and welcome such missionary initiative.

As on the council estates, the Christian congregations in the inner city are often without a church building, not because none have been built but because the large edifices of the past are no longer supportable by the new and often tiny Christian presence. The parish of St Augustine, Halifax, has moved full circle within the past century. It began as a house-church among the new weaving mills. Then a benefactor gave land and a schoolroom was erected. Some time later a Victorian Gothic church appeared, large enough for 700, and, as the present incumbent has said, the anxieties of maintenance began to replace the enthusiasm of mission. As the hundred years drew to an end, mills began to close and terrace houses to crumble. All the more able inhabitants moved out, including those who might have kept the church in repair, and the new Pakistani factory workers, desperate for housing, moved in. But the nucleus of the old St Augustine's congregation, fired with a new sense of fellowship and mission, decided to remain together as a parish after their church had been demolished. The large vicarage, an aided school and a school house provide an adequate centre for their community life. Sunday worship is back where it was 100 years ago – in the school hall. Midweek communicants in various homes usually outnumber those on Sundays. The former study of the vicarage, refashioned as 'The Chapel of the Holy Spirit', is the scene every morning of an hour's group contemplation. Other downstairs rooms have been surrendered for the use of a play group and various meetings. The vicar and his family occupy the first floor. The vicarage attic and the old school house are used to give hospitality to lonely or depressed people who have sought refuge and fellowship. Through the school warm and friendly links are forged with the immigrant families, and the vicar visited towns and villages in Pakistan for a month in order to understand their faith and culture better. As the derelict sites are repopulated, the church family remembers its continued possession of the field on which the church formerly stood, and here also the question is asked: to build or not to build?

Related to this renewal of true mission in the inner city, with its dynamic fusion of witness with social and political involvement, is the unremitting, uphill struggle of those engaged in Industrial Mission. Cast originally in the role of shop floor padres, where many managements would still like to confine them, the chaplains are increasingly seeing their task as a theological one. The world of work is essentially the sphere of the big institutions and the big interests which leave very few options open to purely individual moral choices. Industrial Mission is that realistic arm of the Church which recognizes that a gospel of salvation for modern man cannot be privatized and must have something to say to the big institutions and the big interests. Forty years' experience, from the early beginnings among the French worker-priests, has gained for Industrial Mission both the right and the skill to ask the questions which the gospel raises. The seminar, the broadsheet and, above all, the invited informal consultation, are the main tools of the chaplains today. They are concerned with justice and the Kingdom of God, but they are not in the business of taking sides, since 'taking sides' is itself one of those features of the world of work which they have to question. The furrow they plough is still a lonely one because so many of the parochial clergy have grown up in their ministry believing that the only questions the gospel asks are personal ones. Without realizing it, such clergy are the

victims of our economic structure, which finds it advantageous to
privatize religion in order that it shall not raise questions about the
morality of systems and institutions; so they are naturally out of
sympathy with an approach to the Christian mission which brings
this wider dimension into play. But happily – and here is another
very significant sign of new growth – clergy and laity together are
moving into a much clearer understanding of how the whole of
human life in all its aspects and all its relationships is included
within the judgement and the salvation of God. We have, in fact,
begun to recover the unity of the theology of the cross with the
theology of the Kingdom.

Because we have become more clear about this and more
articulate and confident in saying it, much of the arid argument of
the 1960s has come to an end. This has cleared the way for a far
more positive presentation of Christian faith on television and
radio. Instead of those dreary 'talking heads', the best producers
today are engaging all the resources of their craft to communicate
in as lively a manner as possible the joy, honesty and compassion of
the Christian way of life. Very ordinary believers are allowed to
say what matters to them without arch or obtrusive interviewing.
Radicals and sceptics are given the opportunity to present their
arguments free from the whiff of impending heresy trials. Where
exceptional service is being given in the name of religion it is
treated as straight documentary, neither sentimental nor snide.
Worship of many different types is presented sympathetically and
in such a way as to invite participation. Religious drama is of a high
standard, often penetrating and provocative. There is still, unhap-
pily, the occasional series of what a journalist friend of mine calls
'spiritual pornography', but recent years have shown a steady bias
towards integrity and the ring of truth. The Churches, for their
part, seem at last to be grasping the immense evangelistic potential
of the mass media, and to be doing so without the crude, 'hard sell'
rhetoric of the fundamentalist networks.

It is no disrespect to our great cathedrals that talk of the mass
media leads me to think also of their new forms of ministry as a
similar point of growth in the evangelistic outreach of the Church.
The unbroken rhythm of prayer day by day throughout the year,

the *opus Dei*, remains their primary task, but now it is being seen, both in itself and in its setting, as a powerful witness to the multitudes that have only a vestigial memory of such things. The tourist industry, so-called, brings vaster numbers to these shrines than they have ever known before, and many people who are on or beyond the fringes of the Church and owe no allegiance to a particular local congregation let their motorcar mobility and a Sunday morning whim bring them to a place where they are sure the worship will be impressive and themselves unknown. Not all cathedrals are in this league, but those that are, together with other ancient abbey churches, have an unprecedented opportunity of communicating the forgotten factor, the reality of God. The clergy responsible for such places have begun to give top priority to this side of their ministry. They will fulfil it best not by turning the cathedrals into places of public entertainment or gimmickry, but by continuing to let them be what they are, with a new sensitiveness towards the minds and hearts of those for whom it is totally strange. This calls for a different kind of awareness and sense of purpose and devotion in vergers, guides, bookstall keepers and those who make themselves pastorally available during the hours of sightseeing. Many a tourist comes in to stare or merely to tick off another ancient monument from his list, and finds himself telling his personal problem or anxiety to a complete stranger who has simply asked him with sufficient sympathy whether he is enjoying his visit. The cathedral has overwhelmed him with its truth and healing. This is an asset which is once again coming into its own and the Church is learning to use it with more skill.

I have just used the word 'healing' in connection with the Church's outreach to those who are beyond its fringe. Thirty years ago it would not have occurred to me to do so. But then, thirty years ago many people would have drawn a sharp distinction between the gospel and social action. Far more Christians today have begun to grasp the connection between salvation and wholeness. The agelong pattern of grace, repentance, faith, deliverance and transformation is intended for human life in all its aspects and all its relationships. The process of salvation is just as likely to begin with the reconciliation of a quarrel or a change of policy by a company chairman or the healing of a chronic illness as with a conscious turning to God. It would, in fact, be truer to say that any one of those things may actually *be* a turning to God. This clearer vision of the indivisible wholeness of man's life has enabled the Church to recover an understanding of its ministry of healing which it had well nigh lost. It is widely agreed today that many kinds of sickness — far more than we had supposed — are able to get a grip on us because something has caused the unity of our personal being to fall apart, and we are at war within ourselves. If someone is at enmity with his or her body, making it a source of discontent or disgust, the poor rejected body is deprived of a large part of its vitality and resistance to disease. If we have memories that hurt so much that we have to push them into our unconsciousness in order to make life bearable, we set up a process of anxiety which introduces an unnatural tenseness in the body that may start all kinds of malfunction. The ministry of healing is the sacramental means by which God gives back to us the grace of wholeness. Through prayer and the Eucharist, through the laying on of hands or anointing with oil, negative forces, both personal and social, such as loneliness, humiliation, fear or self-hatred, are held back sufficiently to give the individual's life-giving resources a chance, and at the same time to augment those resources with an influx of confidence and vitality from the risen Christ himself.

A very important sign of new growth in the life of the Church in England is to be seen in congregations where formerly healing was neither practised nor discussed, but in which this ministry now forms an accepted part of the proclamation and presentation of the whole gospel. Though there is undoubtedly a 'gift of healing' which certain people possess in a higher degree than others, this is best exercised in the context of a 'ministry of healing' which belongs to the worshipping community as a whole. There is still some mistrust, confusion and hesitancy, which is not surprising when one considers the history of this ministry. It has been so long neglected that when realization and reaction come they may take the form of unbalanced enthusiasm, issuing in an ill-considered concentration on physical cures isolated from a concern for wholeness in depth which includes personal forgiveness, healing of relationships, and oneness with Christ. These distortions are most likely to be corrected as the Church recovers the ministry of healing as a normal and regular feature of its life. To take as an example our own diocese, which is far from *avant garde* in this matter, the subject of healing is being discussed in youth fellowships, Mothers' Union, house-groups, Parochial Church Councils, parish meetings, deanery chapters, in-service training and Councils of Churches, and, in step with several other dioceses, there is now an episcopal blessing of oils on Maundy Thursday for use in the healing ministry.

There is one common feature of this development which will serve to introduce what, in my view, is the most vigorous and promising of all the signs of growth that are evident in the English church scene. A few years ago a priest might have asked how he should set about this ministry of healing in his own parish. The question now being asked by parishioners and priest together is, 'What is *our* ministry of healing in this parish?' In those churches where this ministry takes place normally in the course of the Parish Eucharist, a small number of selected lay people join the priest in the sanctuary for the laying on of hands with prayer for those who wish to receive it. This is typical of a new movement of lay participation in all aspects of the life and ministry of the Church. As one takes a more distant view of the setting up of synodical government, the out-working of the Pastoral Measure, and especially the long process of liturgical revision, the details that were so hotly argued seem less important and one recognizes that what it has all been about is lay participation in worship and lay responsibility for decision-making.

The heated argument over language and style has blinded us to the really significant thrust of the new service books. What they have achieved at point after point is the incorporation of the nave into the sanctuary. The Eucharist is clearly seen to be the action of the whole people of God. So also is the baptism and confirmation of new members. I do not personally agree with those who complain that this change has been brought about at the expense of a sense of mystery and transcendence, but those who make this criticism are at least focusing their attention upon the real nub of liturgical reform, and insofar as they are right we should try to bring back awe and adoration without losing the fresh theological insights we have so recently gained.

   Lay participation in worship no longer means a few unordained persons trying to resemble clergymen as closely as possible in order to take over marginal parts of the priestly ministry. Lay men and lay women who offer today to read the Scriptures, lead the intercessions, bring bread and wine to the altar and assist in administering the Communion want to do so as representatives of the laity and to look the part. I commend the practice of at least one of the Anglican Archbishops in Australia who, whenever he authorizes lay people to assist in administering the Elements, requires them to wear decent secular dress, not ecclesiastical robes. For the same reason those whose turn it is to bring forward the bread and wine for the Eucharist find that this becomes an even more significant act if they have brought them to the church from their own homes. I quote from an incumbent in north London who is by no means untypical:

> I was soon to realise that underneath the gloom there was in the church an awareness, a liveness and, in fact, a latent exuberance, bursting to come out. Until nine years ago only the priest and the layreaders were ever heard during a service, except very occasionally. Now my lesson readers number 56, those who have expressed a desire to take part in the offertory procession number over 70, and the donors of bread and wine number as many as the number of Sundays in the year and more (for Ascension Day, Ash Wednesday, Maundy Thursday, All Souls' Day, Patronal and Dedication Festivals). The result is that whole families come to church. We are planning to extend this sharing of responsibility to other matters as well, such as keeping the church and hall in good repair, redecoration, providing transport for the aged and the handicapped, etc.

As lay people learn to take this degree of responsibility in public worship when the vicar is present, they realize that they need not be reduced to helpless inaction when he is absent. The three, four or more parishes which make up a united benefice need not prune back their rota of services to the number that one ordained man can cram into a Sunday by tearing from place to place. In many such parishes Readers are certainly not regarded as 'second best', and in the absence of a Reader the churchwardens and other trusted members of a local congregation take it upon themselves to lead the rest in reading Morning or Evening Prayer. This needs only a little more official encouragement and some simple locally-based training in the necessary skills to become normal in all such benefices. Even in large one-church parishes the capacity of the central congregation to draw people in may be augmented by area family services held in school-rooms, church halls or private homes and conducted by lay pastors authorized by the parochial church council and trained by the incumbent. This mention of 'family services', incidentally, deserves notice as another significant growing-point, symptomatic of the movement of lay participation. It may seem ironical that during the years when the General Synod of the Church of England was devoting so much of its time to the revision of its official liturgies the use of more unfixed patterns of worship should have been growing in importance. This explosion of informality has been more marked in Evangelical parishes, but is by no means confined to them. They have usually started in good faith as a simplified service for children with a pre-ponderance of hymns and choruses, a simple talk and a mixture of formal and extempore prayer. But the parents who come osten-sibly to accompany the children often find this form of worship more accessible, and clergy, recognizing this, have adapted their aim to include these adults as well. At their best family services are no longer children's services but acts of worship in which everyone from seven or eight years and upwards, especially those who are totally new to the Christian way, can participate easily. They are nearly always thematic, and in many parishes have become the main means of introducing whole families for the first time to regular Christian worship and teaching. Un-Anglican though it is, this movement is one of the most obvious signs of growth in the Church of England today.

But to return to the development of lay participation — it is not confined to church services. I have already mentioned the growing use of 'lay pastors', or 'elders', as they are sometimes misleadingly called. This is only one of the many ways in which ordinary members of the congregation are taking a deliberate share in the pastoral, evangelistic and managerial tasks that were in the past so often left to the ordained man. I have already quoted the priest on the council estate who finds such delight in seeing diffident and inarticulate people growing into powers of leadership through taking on the organization of a parish lunch. In every part of the country parishes are reporting the same thing.

> Social events are held periodically and the refreshments are provided not by the faithful few but by everyone on the Electoral Roll who are approached by the chairman of our Worship and Fellowship Committee with a letter from me, on a rota basis, so that no one family is expected to bring anything again in three years at least![1]

It is becoming much more common for parochial church councils to spend as much time considering their *spiritual* task in the parish as they give to the discussion of maintenance and management. Some incumbents are able to use every member of their P.C.C. in a pastoral capacity, giving each of them the charge of a different area in the parish. It is, I believe, in the light of this development that we should regard the new 'concessions' granted to churchwardens and parochial church councils over their right to be consulted about an appointment to a vacancy. It is not to be regarded as an awkward legality but a welcome outcome of this new movement of lay participation which offers such hope for the future.

This must all be seen in close relation to another very significant development, namely the emergence of small, human-sized groups as the milieu in which many Christians experience what it means to be the Church. I have already mentioned those careful studies of church growth which have shown conclusively that when a church congregation numbers 120 to 150 it has reached the optimum level for that kind of experience of worship, reflection and fellowship which people are seeking when they attach themselves on a regular basis to a particular church. If the number rises, as many people begin to leave as come in, or the congregation becomes an audience of unattached visitors. The parishes which are steadily drawing in the greatest number of genuinely new members are those which offer, in addition to the Sunday congregation in church, smaller units of fellowship related either to a neighbourhood or to a common interest. We can use the name 'house group' as a general inclusive term, but they may meet in other places than one of the homes of the parish. I know, for example, of three such groups meeting regularly and separately in County Hall, London, one for a simple celebration of Holy Communion, another to discuss questions arising from their daily work, and a third that has recently been looking at the Parables and their present-day relevance. Another group of twelve people, all working in offices around London Bridge, some of whom are committed church members, others not, have come together for a sandwich lunch for a number of years, and the topics they have recently discussed range from patriotism, death, the trade unions, to the World Council of Churches and the meaning of the word 'God'. The man who has been providing their meeting place has remarked on the change which has taken place in the depth of their understanding of themselves and their relationship with the Christian Church. A group to which my wife and I have belonged for fourteen years consists of between ten and twelve people, some married couples and some single, who live as far apart as London, Gloucestershire and Somerset, and meet twice a year for a weekend in the home of one or another of our number. We usually discuss a book which we have read beforehand, but our talk ranges very freely and the moments of new insight and growth are always unforeseeable. The programme of the weekend starts with a devotional meditation and includes a Eucharist on Sunday morning and a separate period of intercession. In the intervals between our meetings we keep a simple rule of weekly communion, short daily meditation, and prayer for each other. For each of us the phrase 'our church' must include our membership of this group alongside any involvement we may have in a local parish.

Clergy at last are beginning to feel less threatened by this development and more and more of them are deliberately fostering the formation of house churches as a normal element in the structure of the local church. The wisest of them support and

guide the group leaders without dictating the methods or the programme they should follow. They offer their help, especially in the
delicate operation of persuading a group to separate into two when
its numbers have increased beyond about twelve or fifteen; for,
like church congregations, house-groups also have their optimum
size beyond which they become static and cease to be growing-
points. The clergy also have the task of representing the wider
Church and fellowship to each small unit, thus saving it from
becoming a self-contained clique. In this way the clergy are taking
upon themselves once again the characteristically apostolic task of
being the 'link-men' who knit together the various local
manifestations of the Church and guard the catholicity of the
whole. But in doing this they would be well-advised not to make
their guidance too structured. I cannot but admire the parish which
issues duplicated study outlines for each of the thirty-five groups
which meet for regular Bible reading – yet I fear it has not really
understood the nature of the house-group movement and is likely
to inhibit its potential growth. For small groups do their most vital
work when they are open to people who are only on the fringe of
the Church and who are attracted by the freedom to explore and
question without being confronted with cut-and-dried answers
they are expected to learn. They meet as human beings rather than
as card-carrying members of a particular denomination. They
meet as people who take each other seriously, whatever their
position or point of view may be, and who take the subject under
discussion seriously. They meet in deepening trust and mutual care
for one another which emboldens them to drop their defences and
expose themselves in honest self-discovery. All of this provides the
ambience in which growth into Christ takes place. I cannot
emphasize too strongly that this is not a modern technique of
group dynamics, though it can certainly be analysed in such terms;
it is the God-given *koinonia* which is as old as the gospel itself. Like
the new wine of the Kingdom, therefore, it is bound to strain the
old wine-skins of order and orthodoxy. House churches become
ecumenical, not by planning but because denominational affilia-
tion is almost irrelevant to their life. The process of *doing* theology
cannot be neatly programmed because it involves sharing and

valuing many different insights and experiences. We need to remember that a lot of those who sit in the pews on Sunday are in a wilderness concerning their personal faith, and the freedom and depth of a house-group discussion can be an oasis from which they drink greedily. Of course they must be given some content for their speculation, but whenever a group is presented with a great biblical theme or motif – redemption, covenant, vineyard, Kingdom – the members contribute profound insights, even those who are least familiar with the Church, if they are only given time. They must be given *time* to reflect and to share, and this is what they cannot be given during a liturgical service in a normal congregation.

If we are looking for signs of new growth, therefore, we must expect to find some of them beyond the circle of what is commonly regarded as the Church. If the main stem of a tree is dying back new shoots will sometimes break through the ground so far from the centre that it is hard to believe they are actually sprung from the old root. 'If a tree is cut down', says the Book of Job, 'there is hope that it will sprout again and fresh shoots will not fail. Though its roots grow old in the earth, and its stump is dying in the ground, if it scents water it may break into bud and make new growth like a young plant' (14. 7–9 NEB). That text has been taken as the framework of a paper written with great passion by Rosemary Haughton, the Roman Catholic lay-theologian and author, about the emergence of a great number of experiments in community living of one sort or another. These are, as it were, a more radical extension of the principle of the house church. People of various ages, but predominantly young, have been committing themselves to live together in some form of shared life as a protest against the cult of bigness and impersonal power, and as an affirmation of the value of being in a group small enough for people to relate to each other directly and humanly. All these experiments in community living have recognized, at least implicitly, that they are up against something basically and finally corrupt and corrupting in modern society. There are those which seek an alternative economic pattern, emphasizing simplicity of life and low consumption. Others are concerned primarily with conservation in all its aspects. Many concentrate on a more therapeutic aim, fostering the human potential of each person by creating an atmosphere of mutual care and trust and by welcoming those who are inadequate for, or damaged by, the pressures of society. Some communities are overtly political in emphasis, some have a predominantly educational aim, and some start with a specifically religious motivation. The failure rate is high because many people who venture into such experiments are not prepared to go through the successive stages of deepening interaction which growth in community requires.

What Rosemary Haughton has observed and described in her paper is the frequency with which groups which were not begun with any specifically religious commitment have, in fact, developed from 'non-church' into 'church'.

> The 'pre-church' is the stage at which a group of people gather together for any number of reasons, and as they interact over a period of time discover a sense of group identity as people involved in some kind of quest, however vaguely articulated. They may come together for one single cause, but if the group is to become a 'pre-church' it will soon diversify the things it does together so as to include the areas of *prayer*, *study* and *action*. In the 'pre-church' situation, the idea of prayer may not be explicit, but there must be a desire to reflect deeply, both personally and in common, on the underlying values which have drawn the group together. . . . A 'pre-church' becomes a 'church' at the moment at which it becomes consciously aware that its identity as a group finds its name, centre and meaning in Christ. This may happen quite suddenly, as it did to the household of Cornelius, or over a long period as Christian words and ideas, vaguely and perhaps uncomfortably heard and used, gradually acquire meaning through their relation to activities and common experiences, and little by little words and experiences become linked, until people begin to say 'Jesus' and mean not just somebody in a story, nor an ideal, but an effective presence and fact. The theological articulation of the awareness of Jesus as the 'being' of the group may be rudimentary or naive, or even falsely stated, but although this may lead to mistakes or disaster later, such inadequacies do not alter the fact that this is the one single event which creates a *church*. No amount of zeal, heroism and piety will make a church without the conscious recognition of Christ as its

meaning, and no failure or one-sidedness in the group will alter the fact that it *is* a church, once this recognition has occurred.

A realistic reading of church history leads one to expect, I am afraid, that the Church which has become one of the big institutions will be unlikely to recognize, cherish and learn from these living manifestations of its own future. Yet one must go on praying, hoping and taking all possible action to forge links of sympathy and awareness between the old Church and the new form of Christian fellowship. It can be done and the house church, firmly based within the life of the parish, may often be the bridge. Boldness is our need, and trust. This is where the renewal movement, charismatic or catholic, will play its most significant part. I have deliberately not included either of these renewal movements among the specific signs of growth mentioned in this chapter. They belong to a different category. Neither charismatic revival nor catholic renewal can, in themselves, ensure that a local church will learn the ways of communicating with the dwellers on a council estate or in an inner city or make a reality of lay participation. Renewal in some places only entrenches conservatism. But, at its best, renewal of any sort brings a new-found courage, and this is what is needed so that the Church may embrace and make its own each of the new shoots that are appearing all around. At the height of the Black Death in the fourteenth century the Church in England lost half its priests – a decimation enormously greater than anything we are likely to suffer in this century. Yet it was at that moment that Bishop William of Edington and Bishop William of Wykeham introduced the daring modernity of the Perpendicular style into the massive Norman nave of Winchester, and Wykeham built his school and college to nurture a new style of clergy. It has ever been so; when there is most cause for despondency the Spirit points out the breaking buds of the future. They are there in plenty in England today.

NOTE

1. 'There is hope for a tree', a study paper on the Emerging Church, by Rosemary Haughton. Reproduced by permission of the author.

TWO

Signs of Growth

A view from the Northern Province

—————

The Right Reverend COLIN JAMES,

Bishop of Wakefield, formerly Canon of Winchester and Bishop Suffragan of Basingstoke

The beauty and antiquity of Winchester have long moved men's hearts and fired their imaginations. The ninth centenary celebrations of the Cathedral in July 1979 were richly evocative of the faith and vision which inspired its building. Walking past my former home in the Close, looking up at the massive garden wall which once formed part of the Norman minster, and then gazing at St Swithun's tomb, it must be admitted that twentieth-century Wakefield and the industrialized West Riding seemed somewhat remote.

Despite their present great diversity the two dioceses of Winchester and Wakefield trace their spiritual origins to Augustine's Canterbury. Pope Gregory's mission, which despatched Birinus to be bishop of the West Saxons in 634, had sent Paulinus to Yorkshire a decade earlier. Indeed Paulinus preached and baptized in 627 in Dewsbury, now the central point of the Wakefield diocese.

Wakefield is one of the most industrialized of the English dioceses. In the eastern half lie the coal mines of West and (in part) South Yorkshire; while towards the Pennines the long-established textile industry, based on Halifax, Huddersfield and Dewsbury, survives, though much reduced in size and in the process of modernization. In recent years smaller light industries have provided jobs for people who once would have worked in the mills. And the population has been augmented by a sizeable immigrant community from Pakistan, India and (to a lesser extent) the West Indies.

By 1888, when the Wakefield diocese was founded, the heroic

expansionist period of Victorian Christianity had passed its peak, although none realized this at the time. The available statistics are not particularly reliable nor always easy to interpret. While the numbers of baptisms, confirmations and (almost certainly) of communicants in England increased in the last two decades of the century, the number of worshippers did not rise in proportion to the general growth of the population. Moreover, in the 1890s there was a decline in the level of ordinations and fewer new churches were being built. By 1900 there was an actual decrease of church-going in the great northern towns (where the hold of the Church of England was not so strong as in the south), and it was very apparent that working men did not figure substantially in church or chapel congregations. At the beginning of this century occasional voices were heard to declare that the tide of revival was beginning to ebb.[1]

In the past eighty years, especially since 1960, that tide has gone out a very long way indeed. England is no longer an avowedly Christian nation, though its folk religion has certain Christian attachments; equally the nation is not avowedly secularist. In 1980 the remedies and beliefs of politicians, economists, social reformers, and secular humanists too, are greeted with a scepticism that Christians have long been accustomed to.

There are now some indications that intelligent people are willing to take religious issues more seriously than would have been likely only a few years ago. When Professor Hans Küng, Dr Schillebeeckx and the Dutch bishops are called to account in Rome the issues are widely reported and discussed. In the past decade, when Europe's political and cultural self-confidence has been considerably impaired, the role of the papacy and its hold on men's imagination has significantly increased.

It would be a mistake to read too much into this. There are fashions in philosophy and spirituality as in much else. The failure of confidence in human self-sufficiency does not necessarily portend a theological renaissance or a religious revival. What it does indicate is that the position is now rather more open than it was. There are signs that there are more people willing to consider Christian faith and life seriously than there were.

When Archbishop Ramsey retired in 1974 he spoke of the Church being smaller, less secure but more lively than in the past. 'Lively' in the biblical sense, with the presence of the Spirit of God. There are many who would echo this, and see around them signs of hope and growth.

What follows is inevitably subjective and impressionistic. The canvas is small, drawn from a traditional rather than trend-setting diocese. I am aware that things which are growing bravely but only in a small way in West Yorkshire soil have been longer established and are more luxuriant in other places, where the climate is softer and the soil perhaps more fertile.

Of the two hundred or so parishes in the diocese, the overwhelming majority are served by dedicated and frequently too hard working priests. In England every citizen is resident in a parish and has a rightful claim on the services of his parish priest for ministry, particularly for baptisms, marriages and funerals. Although only a proportion avail themselves of it, and a still smaller proportion make any financial commitment to the Church, the pastoral demands on the priest for such a ministry – beyond the confines of the congregation – can be taxing, particularly where a man is single-handed in a large parish. Most priests are supported by bands of faithful, committed lay people, who in their quiet way love and serve their Lord and cherish their church.

In 1980 we initiated (in common with some other dioceses) a diocesan pattern of renewal. We have not sought to programme the activity of the Holy Spirit, nor to devise a blueprint for the parishes. We began with a Lent course of sermons on the five essentials of Christian life:

Worship
Pastoral Care and Fellowship with one another
Learning as the Christian family
Witness through living and sharing the Good News
Service of the local community.

House and study groups examined these same five essentials. Each parish was invited to undertake a simple 'Know your Church' and

also a 'Know your Neighbourhood' survey, so that the teaching of
the sermons and the findings of the house groups could be properly
earthed. We encouraged each congregation to hold a special
meeting at Whitsuntide for prayer, study and assessment, leading
to action, on the immediate priorities in the life of the parish, and
to see under God how they might be tackled. What is God calling
us to be and do?

Inevitably the response to this kind of initiative is patchy.
Parishes vary in their tradition, location and composition, and also
in confidence. Each parish is unique. And much depends on where
a parish has got to, how it sees itself, and on the work it already has
in hand. The majority have accepted this initiative as a re-
enforcement of a movement that is already taking place.

To assist the parishes we formed a number of working parties, to
explore what is already proving to be significant in worship,
evangelism, pastoral care, parish education and social responsibility. In this way useful experience can be more widely known
and readily shared. Resource material can be made available for
parishes to use or adapt as they seek to grow in the way they
believe God is calling them.

The underlying conviction of this diocesan initiative is that
Christianity is a movement involving every lay person, and that
the Body of Christ in each locality should accept its shared responsibility under God for developing the life and mission of the
Church in its own area.

That this understanding requires a considerable change in the inherited attitudes of Anglican lay people cannot be denied, and on
the part of some of the clergy too. Yet there are signs that this shift
is already taking place, and that it is spreading.

Twenty parishes immediately come to mind where lay education and ministry are now taken very seriously. Some of these have
been graciously influenced by the renewal movements, though not
all of them could be described as 'charismatic' parishes. They vary:
evangelical, catholic, central church. Their situations vary too:
local authority housing estate, urban, suburban, down-town and
rural. Their worship is attentive yet relaxed, liturgical and par-
ticipatory. They experience and express a deepened sense of com-

mitment to our Lord, and of mutual concern for one another.
Their congregations are growing. Alongside them there are a considerable number of parishes which have a long tradition of sound
teaching and ordered worship, which are continuing to develop
both well-tried and new ways of making effective witness and of
using the gifts that are to be found within their membership.

In two or three parishes there are lay leadership teams. The
patterns are flexible. In one parish, a thinking and planning group
of the wardens, the Readers, and one or two teachers meet weekly
for prayer and discussion; while in the same parish a group of
pastoral visitors call regularly on those who are on the electoral
roll. Meanwhile an administrative group superintends the church's
programme and publicity. In other parishes, the lay leadership
roles are not so clearly differentiated, but there are teams exer-
cising the same kind of responsibility. From an interesting cross-
section of parishes men and women are beginning to offer
themselves for training for local ministry – as visitors, counsellors,
teachers, group leaders or administrators. Some of these volunteers
have only recently been confirmed, and it is noteworthy that a
third of our confirmation candidates are adults.

There are several dioceses which have well-established schemes
for lay ministry training, while we are only at the planning stage.
We hope to benefit from the experience of the pioneers in this
area, and to foster lay ministry training courses in the deaneries.

Most of our parishes have house groups which meet regularly
for bible study, prayer and discussion. A few abound with such
groups, having a dozen or more. Their value is considerable in
deepening personal and spiritual growth. Members gain a surer
grasp of the Christian faith; they learn to be more open with each
other and they experience a deep sense of fellowship. And the
variety of groups, for teaching and training, for caring and
evangelism, enriches the quality of parish life.

It has long been known that certain parishes, usually through the
influence of outstanding incumbents, have a tradition of producing
ordination candidates. This remains true, but we are also finding
that it is in the parishes where house-groups are effective and
where lay ministry is being exercised that men and women are

coming forward to test their vocation to the priesthood or as deaconesses and licensed lay workers. Historically the Wakefield diocese has been an importing rather than an exporting diocese for young priests. We may now be beginning to see signs of a reversal. In 1979 our Candidates Panel, which advises the bishop on sponsoring men and women for ACCM selection conferences, interviewed twenty-seven people offering themselves for the priesthood, and six candidates for women's ministry.

Those who came forward include:

A family man in his middle thirties, holding a senior post as production manager in an engineering firm, enthusiastically backed by his parish.

A married scientific graduate, working for his Ph.D., coming to Christian faith while at the University.

A young man from a broken home, who became a Christian in his teens, with a great capacity for making pastoral contacts with non-church people.

A psychiatric nurse who is a Reader and belongs to a lay leadership team.

A mature university graduate, now in his mid-thirties, holding a research fellowship to read for a further degree.

A personable twenty-year-old, who has been on Christian service attachments in India and with the Church Army.

The head of a department in a large comprehensive school, who feels a call to stipendiary ministry.

A married man in his thirties in middle management, encountering difficult problems of reconciling personal loyalties with professional and ethical standards.

To a large extent the variety of gifts and experience that these men (and the women candidates also) bring is being evoked and exercised in the local church in the first instance. As we recognize and then mobilize the gifts for shared ministry in each parish, the body of Christ becomes more active through all its members in its own immediate setting. Far from minimizing the priestly office by magnifying shared lay ministry, it is precisely through the development of a more widely-ranging lay ministry that God is calling men and women for ordained and professional ministry in the wider Church.

Our Diocesan Education Department has been fostering this broad-based understanding of service and witness through its Parish Education Programme for Ministry and Mission. It provides a core course on the basics of Christian faith, and various practical options on either the work of the parish, youth studies (for those working with young people), or prayer and spiritual growth. This pattern is offered in different centres of the diocese. Those who take part value the stimulus, and it also helps to reinforce the development of lay ministry in the parishes which have been involved.

The Dewsbury deanery has devised a far-reaching lay training course under the leadership of a resident deaconess. There are weekly meetings in terms of six successive weeks, over a two or three year period. The course is repeated in three parish centres. The evening sessions last for two and a half hours, beginning with a talk (followed by questions) for the first forty-five minutes. After the coffee-break there are workshops conducted by local clergy or invited experts on some practical aspects of church life.

In the first term the talks give an introduction to the Bible: how it was written and handed down, and the kinds of documents it contains. The aim is to give background information so that people can use the Bible more confidently at home and in parish life. Students are given notes to take away as a permanent record, and there are bible readings for them to do if they wish. The workshops in this term are concerned with the functioning church member:

participation in public worship
worship in the home
contact with overseas missionary societies
his place in synodical government
money matters
church buildings

From this general introduction the course concentrates on more specific aspects of teaching and church life in the following terms:

Talks	Workshops
Life with the early Christians — an introduction to the Epistles	Parish Groups
Church History and the Denominations	Matters of debate and conflict in the Church today, e.g. marriage and baptism discipline
The life and teaching of Jesus	Evangelism — Stage 1 — people going out — visiting and witnessing
Problems for belief—e.g. miracles, inspiration of the Bible, etc.	Evangelism — Stage 2 — people coming in — how we can use the opportunities when people approach us in church clubs or for occasional offices
Christian belief (a look at major themes of the Creed)	The Church in the community

It is a highly ambitious programme of systematic teaching and practical ministry. The course has been well supported in the different deanery centres, and some of those taking part describe it as their most valuable learning experience as adult Christians.

Christian adult education is still a rare and tender plant. Much has yet to be done to establish healthy growth and to persuade people that it is necessary and desirable. It is only as people in the parishes become aware of their need for such education and are motivated to seek it that anything far-ranging will happen. We are as yet only at the beginning.

In the more formal educational structures there are a number of encouraging developments. The diocese has fifty-one voluntary aided and seventy-eight voluntary controlled day schools at first and middle levels and one voluntary aided senior school. We have regular consultations for head teachers, for clergy with church schools in their parishes, and for school managers. In the Cathedral we have special services with full participation by the children from our schools, and a growing number of schools come to visit the Cathedral. Our Director of Education is mounting a series of workshops on the new diocesan syllabus, and there are courses for non-specialist teachers in church and local authority schools on the use of the Bible in religious education. The diocesan education department has created an impressive resource centre of 3,000 books, kits, tapes and films which can be used in schools and parishes.

The Sunday schools in the north of England have traditionally been much stronger than those in the south. It came as a surprise to me three years ago to discover that some parishes had actual buildings adjacent to the church called the Sunday School. In the last thirty years the vitality and strength of the Sunday School has diminished here as elsewhere. But parishes and parents alike are coming to recognize the need for the local church to provide adequate Christian teaching for their children and young people, because the provision in the state school system has so greatly changed its emphasis. In 1978 our diocesan Director of Education inaugurated a postal course for Sunday School teachers, supplemented by the help of local tutors and termly diocesan training days. To gain their Diocesan Certificate the teachers undertake to do ten weeks' work each term for a year. Once a fortnight they receive a package of study notes, booklists and audio-visual material, and are given practical assignments to complete. In the first term they concentrate on the aims and organization of the Sunday School, the understanding of the child's world and growth, and his context in family, school and church. During the second term the teacher is concerned with work-content – planning a syllabus, preparing lessons, teaching Scripture, growth in prayer. And in the final term different educational methods are explored – child-centred and thematic approaches, dance and drama, children and worship, and the presentation of material. The course makes big demands on the teachers, who are responding well and in growing numbers.

Following the publication of the Albemarle Report there was in the 1960s an awakened interest in young people's work. Most dioceses appointed their youth officers to help with church clubs and groups and to make links with clubs run by local authorities. In recent years much of this momentum has been lost. Although the uniformed organizations like the Scouts and Guides have maintained and increased their strength, other youth organizations have not been so flourishing. Yet significant work in church groups does go on. A recent diocesan youth day for worship, a variety of workshops, and recreation attracted many young people. And the day was enlivened by the presence of the Archbishop of York, who gave a characteristically encouraging and engaging talk that was received with acclaim.

The links of friendship between the Youth departments of Winchester and Wakefield have enabled us to adopt in the north various events for young people such as post-confirmation weekends to our great advantage. Valuable experience is gained by teenagers drawn from various parishes who stay in the homes of the host parish, meeting others of their own age, planning and sharing in worship, learning more about the Christian faith, doing projects, and taking part in recreational activities.

Not long before he died in 1965, Fr Jonathan Graham, Superior of the Community of the Resurrection, Mirfield (which is situated in the diocese) wrote: 'The revival of the liturgical life throughout Christendom is an ever-growing source of thankfulness; and it must be balanced by an equally adventurous revival in the art of that individual alignment with the will of God, the venture of prayer.'[2] Since Fr Graham wrote those words the parish Eucharist has become the typical act of worship offered on Sunday mornings in the great majority of our churches. Our people have become accustomed to using modern liturgical services, and there is more lay participation both in the Eucharist and in family services than there was a generation ago. There are now heartening signs that the need for the balancing factor, of which Fr Graham wrote, 'the individual alignment with the will of God, the venture of prayer', is being recognized. In the diocese we have reason to be grateful for courses given at Mirfield by Fathers of the Community of the Resurrection.

In the last two years members of the Mothers' Union have come to the Cathedral on Ascension Day for an extended Eucharist and instruction on mental prayer. The Association for the Promotion of Retreats has now formed its own committee for the north. In 1979 it organized a Celebration of Prayer Festival in York, and a shared conference with the Roman Catholic National Retreat Council in Manchester with a fascinating variety of twenty different workshops. Each diocese now has its own A.P.R. representative, with a support group, encouraging the holding of schools of prayer, quiet days, retreats and conferences. Alongside this a number of parishes have residential weekends for prayer, teaching and fellowship. Other groups like the Fellowship of Contemplative prayer, whose leader is a parish priest in the diocese, and the Julian Meetings are providing opportunities for groups to meet for prayer and instruction on a regular or occasional basis. Only a minority of people in a minority of parishes is yet involved, but it is a significant minority from significant parishes of whose spiritual vitality there can be no doubt.

The separation of the spiritual from the material is as congenial to the heart of the average Anglican as it is to the mind of the Manichee. Church of England Man hitherto has expected his religion and his church to be provided for him at minimal cost. Today, I marvel at the way our parishes pay, in full, their annual quotas to central funds. The strenuous efforts they make to do this are additional to meeting the soaring costs of church heating, repairs, maintenance, and insurance and making a realistic attempt to pay in full the incumbent's working expenses. They have shouldered these burdens with astonishing resolve. Yet often it seems it is the offerings of the dedicated few rather than the majority that make these results possible. For many of us, even after twenty years, stewardship comes as a novel and unwelcome threat, best avoided, like a bumper in a cricket field.

It is unfortunate that so often stewardship has been equated with money-raising and thus readily condemned as materialistic. Fundamentally, it is about commitment to God, and the use of personal and corporate resources for the ministry and mission of the Church. These resources include money but also much else.

In the diocese we have been fortunate to have a dedicated layman as our Stewardship Adviser, who goes to a parish not for a money-raising campaign but a stewardship mission. The emphasis is on the growth in the life of the Church, the mobilization of the gifts and resources of the membership for the offering of worship, the work of evangelism, and the fostering of pastoral relationships through home visiting and house-groups. A parish is invited to discover its own needs and opportunities for ministry and mission, and so to realize its own personal and financial resources. A stewardship mission is primarily concerned with the extension of the Kingdom of God and not with preservation and maintenance.

In an analysis of seven stewardship campaigns in 1979 our Adviser calculated the number of people who had offered personal help in various aspects of church life:

264 – in worship (reading, interceding, choir, sidesmen)
44 – in young people's work (with adolescents and Sunday School)
277 – in further training and education (including baptism and confirmation preparation, house-group activities)
402 – in pastoral and evangelistic work
133 – in administration and social work
223 – in maintaining buildings

Yet the real challenge lies in how far these offers are taken up.

In financial terms the results were no less striking: an average increase of 75% in parish income. There were other increases, too:

in the number of people giving regularly　　(32%)
in covenanted giving　　(73%)
in the average family offering per week – from 75p to £1.02

Yet this last figure is misleading. It conceals the fact that a quarter of the congregation families give about double this amount, i.e. £2.02 per week, while the rest give well below the £1.02 average. Despite the encouraging rise in covenanted giving, the financial challenges of stewardship have still to be faced by most of our families. It may well be only as the offers of practical service in the parish are seized that the financial responsibilities will come home to 75% of the members. The tasks of education and motivation have still to go on, and in this the more realistic and committed 25% have an important part to play. However, the General

Synod's initiative in commending the 5% standard of giving is being followed up in this diocese as in others. For the first time the Church as a whole is seeking to change its members' attitudes and help them accept that a significant level of giving is an integral part of personal discipleship. Yet it will take time and love, patience and careful teaching before most of our members will come to adopt the standard, particularly in a period of very severe recession when there is so much insecurity about jobs.

Although stewardship is rightly more addressed to mission, and the realization of potential commitment, than preservation and maintenance, the latter cannot be ignored. A large number of our churches are currently commemorating their 100th or 150th anniversaries: they are the products of the Victorian expansion programme. It is clear that some of these buildings have reached the end of their life span. With others, church councils are starting to examine their continuing suitability as places of worship. They are having to weigh various factors: the condition of the structure, its size, its siting in relation to the neighbourhood and to other churches and halls, its adaptability for modern worship, the costs of insurance, heating, repairs and maintenance, and the ability of the congregation to meet them. Our neighbouring diocese of Bradford has produced a working party report: 'A new life for old buildings'. This sets out useful criteria for parishes to assess the viability of their buildings, what options are open, and how adaptations might be made. In our own diocese there have been several imaginative schemes sensitively reordering the interior of church buildings for modern liturgy, reducing the height and floor space, and incorporating meeting rooms and halls within the main structure. These developments usually follow a careful appraisal of the local church's ministry and mission, and are a response to it.

It has to be acknowledged that as a Church we are better at this kind of internal analysis and action than we are at working out how we might become more effective as corporate agents of the Kingdom of God ministering in and to the world in its needs. And sadly, apart from the heartening personal integrity and witness that Christian laymen and women bring to their daily work, and to voluntary organizations (which are so often though not exclusively served by Christians), there is little to report from the diocese of the Church's corporate engagement with the world.

We badly need to foster opportunities for Christians to meet in settings related to their work, and to create a climate of opinion which will encourage this. Heartening though the signs of growth are in many parishes, there is a danger of our people's involvement becoming too domesticated. Adult education and lay ministry training must avoid being too exclusively orientated towards the local church and thus insufficiently geared to equip men and women to engage as Christians with the issues that concern them in work and society. The residential church with its ordered parish Eucharist or family service, its house-groups, its programme of events, needs to be complemented by the church of the dispersion, untidy, informal, elastic in its groupings, enabling men and women to meet to explore the implication of being Christian and living authentically in the context of their work. Priests and lay people, imaginative, sensitive and intelligent, ought to be thinking and praying as Christian adults where they are fully stretched in daily life. The latent weakness of the local church is shallowness; the food provided for the nourishment of mind and spirit is often insubstantial. The prayers we offer in church and home frequently fail to affirm our work, our relationships and our needs in their complexity and profundity. The local church has to grow in depth, and encourage its members to find ways of encountering the presence and discerning the meaning of Christ in settings related to where they are doing their creative work.

The theological work on industrial mission by such recent writers as Margaret Kane, Dr Haddon Willmer, and John Atherton is fresh and stimulating. The last has stressed the need for involvement with secular structures through selecting particular issues as entry points into the key elements of a situation. It is only through co-operation with those chiefly involved or affected, and a willingness to pursue with them a rigorous analysis of their problems and what underlies them, that any effective Christian word or insight can be brought to bear.[3]

There is one significant area in the diocese where the Church is publicly engaged and involved — community relations. For the past eight years Fr Bernard Chamberlain of the Community of the Resurrection has served as the Bishop's Adviser in this field. In large part his task is educational. He seeks to help the Church and the community at large in schools, offices and factories to welcome and build up the new multi-racial/cultural/religious society. And in this process he sees the Church as a sign of God's community-forming love in the world. Fr Chamberlain has established a wide circle of friends, and has won the trust of many leaders among the immigrant communities. Such bodies as the Kirklees Interfaith Fellowship organize festivals, conferences and social events. In Dewsbury and Wakefield the home tutor schemes (co-ordinated by the wives of two of our incumbents) provide tutors to visit and befriend Asians in their homes, to teach them English language and also about English customs. There is still a great need for more people to volunteer for this work. In the last few years multi-racial house parties have enabled lower income families to stay in the homes of Pateley Bridge parishioners in August. Links with the West Indian Churches in Huddersfield have been formed, leading to a Whitsuntide Festival of Praise. At Woodhall each year a Three Faiths Conference is held with Christian, Jewish and Muslim participation. In Halifax a parish priest (on his return from a visit to Pakistan with Fr Chamberlain) has opened a parish charity shop. It is run by the verger who lives on the premises surrounded on all sides by Pakistani neighbours, and already the shop has become a focal point in the community.

Yet it would be misleading to claim that any or all of these enterprises engage more than a fraction either of Christians or of the immigrant communities. There is still much suspicion and mistrust, and a reluctance on the part of many to become involved with their neighbour. In the field of community relations as in so much else – lay education and ministry, youth work, spiritual devotion and renewal, stewardship, evangelism, industrial mission, ecumenical co-operation, the adaptation of buildings – these are signs of growth, which are real and significant, yet they remain small. They are sufficient, indeed more than sufficient, to engender hope. Our real need is to pray with more confidence and conviction that God will illuminate the minds of his people with his truth, warm our hearts with a greater devotion, and so fortify our wills to serve his Kingdom with more zeal.

NOTES

1. Owen Chadwick, *The Victorian Church*, vol. ii, chapter 5.
2. *The Office of a Wall* (Faith Press), p. 92.
3. John Atherton, *The Mission of the Church and Industry*. William Temple Foundation 1977.

THREE

Signs of Growth in the Church of Scotland

The Very Reverend Dr JOHN R. GRAY,
Minister of Dunblane Cathedral

A habit among undergraduate debaters is to begin by quarrelling with the formulation of the question to be debated. That habit of long past student days may be accepted as excuse for questioning the title of this book. The death of the Church is a possibility for which no Christian need allow. If one sees the ark of the Lord trembling, one may be sure that it is due to a swimming in one's own head. We have the word of Christ that 'the gates of hell shall not prevail' against the Church (Matthew 16. 18 AV). That does not mean that an embattled Church will somehow be able to hold the fort against the attacks of hell. On the contrary, it means what it says: that the gates of hell are already quivering and splintering before the attacks of the army of the living God. 'The kingdoms of this world are become the kingdoms of our Lord, and of his Christ; and he shall reign for ever and ever' (Revelation 11. 15 AV). That might be described by some as sheer simplistic triumphalism, but what is fundamentally more simple than the gospel and who should be more triumphal than the disciples of the risen Christ — the triumphant Conqueror of the last enemy of man?

'Like a mighty army', we sing, 'moves the Church of God.' For a time the mighty army has been confined to barracks, content to sustain few losses. But the time has come for advance. That is the only possible direction for the Church of God. The Church is the Body of Christ and is alive. Everything that lives grows, and everything that grows lives. Since we have the word of Christ for it that the Church cannot die, it must grow.

It is an odd thing, growth — a continual externalization of a potential which has always been there. It obviously fascinated Christ. 'Consider the lilies', he said, not 'how they are in their perfection', but 'how they grow' (Matthew 6. 28 AV). 'The earth bringeth forth fruit of herself; first the blade, then the ear, after that the full corn in the ear' (Mark 4. 28 AV). He constantly saw in the growth of plants and flowers and trees a picture of the growth of the Kingdom of God. 'The Kingdom of God', he said, 'is like a grain of mustard seed which . . . groweth' (Mark 4. 30–32 AV). From a tiny seed to a great tree to shelter the birds of the air – that, he said, is how it will be with the Church. And in the history of the Church his words have proved to be true. There are now 1,100,000,000 Christians in the world where there were but a handful when he died. There are 63,000 converts to Christ every day that dawns. The Church of Scotland, to anticipate, adds 250 young people every week. Any political party would be beyond measure delighted if it could show a hundredth part of that gain. The growth of the Church may not be, indeed is not, continuous. But we should not expect it to be. Every gardener is familiar with the fact that some flowers and vegetables grow for a time, and then seem to rest, before they come away again. Some plants suffer if they are transplanted or if there is a touch of frost. By and by, however, they begin to grow again. So is it with the Church.

When Professor Kenneth Scott Latourette cast around for a title for his compendious history of the Church from the beginning until our own day, he decided that the only appropriate name would be *A History of the Expansion of Christianity*. Admitting an ebb and flow in the life of the Church, he maintained that each ebb was less and each flow greater. So the expansion has continued. It is masked, however, by the fact that the Church does not advance on a broad front throughout the world. At the same time as it seems to stagnate in one area, in another there are great gains. Arthur Hugh Clough's lines apply:

> For while the tired waves, vainly breaking,
>   Seem here no painful inch to gain,
> Far back, through creeks and inlets making,
>   Comes silent, flooding in, the main.

And not by eastern windows only,
  When daylight comes, comes in the light;
In front, the sun climbs slow, how slowly!
  But westward, look, the land is bright!

Thus while, as will be seen later, the Church of Scotland has only been growing slowly and only in certain directions, some of its daughter Churches have been making considerable progress. This is true, for example, of the Church of Central Africa Presbyterian in Malawi. It has been increasing by 10,000 communicants a year. That Church owes its existence to the Church of Scotland and still draws much of its strength from Scotland. In a speech at Blantyre at Easter 1977, Life President Banda spoke of his pride in being an elder of the Church of Scotland and said, 'Without the Church of Scotland there would be no Malawi.' It may be that the older Churches should for a time be willing to use their resources in the Third World where advances are to be made, rather than expend their strength on those in Britain, case-hardened to the gospel – call in the New Countries, as it were, to redress the balances of the Old. We are not bound to see the Church prosper in every country at the same time or at the same speed.

In Britain at the moment capitalist materialism is the dominant philosophy. It has a greater hold than communist materialism has in Russia. It may be that the Church must wait for what the Psalmist calls 'the reproofs of life' to have their dire but salutary effect. For it is only when we have nothing left save God alone that we learn how much we have in him alone. Yet there is in all men a hunger for God, even if it is not always recognized for what it is. There is a great hole in the heart of humanity, and though all the drugs and drink, all the money and entertainment on earth are poured into that hole, they will disappear without a trace. It can be filled by God alone. 'Give me of thyself', said Augustine, 'without which, tho' thou shouldest give me all else that ever thou hast made, yet can I not be satisfied.'

The only alternative to the despair which is ready to engulf every man is faith. The only hope of a saner society is in a revival of religion. The tide of sheer evil – crime, alcoholism, divorce, vandalism – must be stemmed. There are signs of an increasing awareness on the part of many that nothing can stem that tide save the power of God made free in Jesus Christ; and a realization that the ordinary means whereby that power comes into men's lives is through the Church. Lord Home, in his autobiography, *The Way the Wind Blows*, tells how he asked Harold Macmillan if he could put his finger on the point in time when the slide in values in Britain began to set in. The answer came without hesitation: 'The day when people stopped going to church regularly on a Sunday morning.'

We may be thankful, therefore, for the signs in Scotland, at least, of a return to religion, to the worship of God on a Sunday morning. People are becoming aware of their quite desperate need of God and are coming to see that the Church and its services, its fellowship and its sacraments, are essential if that need is to be met.

There are three ways in which growth may be measured:

1. By means of crude totals of membership.
2. By an analysis of these totals, to take account of potential. For example, a school in which the lower forms are much larger than the upper has much more hope of growth than one in which the reverse is true.
3. By taking into account signs of life and adaptability which cannot be measured statistically. For example, most young people in their late teens may be growing in maturity, poise and wisdom in the very years in which they are losing weight.

Before looking at crude totals of communicant membership, it may be worth while to set the scene: Scotland has a population of 5,195,000, of whom 3,536,000 are reckoned to be adults of 20 years of age or over. The ecclesiastical situation in Scotland is completely different from that in England. The Church of Scotland is national in the sense of having complete State recognition. The Sovereign, either in person or by deputy – The Lord High Commissioner – attends each General Assembly, but may speak only when invited to do so. The Sovereign, while, of course, held in the greatest respect, is in no sense Head of the Church of Scotland. The great war cry of the Church in the seventeenth century, 'the Crown Rights of the Redeemer', has never died away. The Church, while national, is therefore completely free, its right to manage its own affairs having been explicitly acknowledged by Act of Parliament in 1921. No appeal may be made to the civil courts or to Parliament from decisions properly come to by the General Assembly. The Church accepts the responsibilities of a territorial ministry and maintains the ordinances of religion even in remote parts of the Highlands and Islands where the population is small and contributions from the people, although generous, fall far short of the costs of maintaining the ministry. The Church of Scotland is and always has been a Church of the people in the sense that its links are with the masses rather than with the classes. In the sixteenth and seventeenth centuries the Kirk allied itself with the people over against Roman Catholic or Episcopalian monarchs. Again in the last two centuries, there has been a tendency for the upper classes to regard things English as somehow more elegant and superior and so to send their sons to English public schools, where many were confirmed as Anglicans. This did not apply among working people or the middle classes, who remained attached to the Church of Scotland.

With the decline of the influence of the landed classes and the growth of working class power, the influence of the Church of Scotland has grown, while that of Churches allied with Tory land-owners diminished. Men like James Brown and Lord Mathers were, and in our own day Dr Dickson Mabon, Gregor Mackenzie and Teddy Taylor are, all elders in the Church. At one and the same time they brought, and bring, the influence of the gospel to bear upon politics and the prestige of high office to their service in the Church. In addition, Calvinism – which was the form in which the Reformation came to Scotland – is essentially democratic. The system of popular election, whereby a minister is chosen by the congregation concerned, forges a closer link between the man chosen and his people than is the case where a clergyman is pre-sented to a parish. The phrase 'Our man' in Scotland is constantly used of the minister and is often used with a wealth of affection and respect. The integration of the Church of Scotland with the whole life of the country was increased in 1929 when it united with the equally strong or stronger United Free Church of Scotland – itself a union of several dissenting bodies. This is as if in England a union had taken place between the various Free Churches and a subsequent union had come about with the Church of England.

A peculiar feature of the Church of Scotland and, as many would see it, its particular strength lies in the eldership. Elders are men – and in recent years a few women – who are ordained for life but who continue in their ordinary occupations. The oversight of each parish is in the hands of the Kirk Session which consists of the minister, who is always moderator or chairman, and at least two elders. In some large parishes there may be seventy or eighty. The Kirk Session meets normally about once a month. It fixes the hours of public worship, decides who shall be admitted as members, supervises the organization of the parish and is responsible for everything except the actual conduct of public worship. Once a month the minister and one elder from each of a number of parishes meet together as a Presbytery – which roughly corresponds to a diocese. The Presbytery supervises the work of the parishes and it is to the Presbytery that the minister is responsible. Like the Kirk Session, it can and does discuss matters of doctrine. It is the Presbytery which ordains ministers to parishes – although only the ministers, the preaching presbyters, take part in the laying on of hands. Once a year the General Assembly meets. Like the Presbytery, it consists half of ministers and half of elders, with a minister as Moderator. It is the supreme court of the Church and can legislate on all matters affecting the life of the Church – although a certain delaying power is allowed to Presbyteries by what is known as the Barrier Act. Elders are drawn from all classes in the community – farmers and fishermen, judges and dukes. In the parish each elder is given a district – a kind of sub-parish – to take care of. In most churches the Holy Communion is celebrated three or four times a year, when a high proportion of the communicant membership, approximating perhaps to half, usually attend on one Sunday, if not actually at one service. These periodic celebrations may be supplemented in some parishes by occasional extra Communion services, but before the principal celebrations the elder takes cards for every member to the households in his district. These cards are returned on Communion Sunday and enable a record to be kept of the attendance of all the members at the Sacrament. The distribution of these Communion cards means that the elder visits each home in his district three or four times a year. A good elder may visit much oftener where he knows that there is sickness or sorrow or other special need.

The number of elders in the Church of Scotland increased from 31,443 in 1921 to a peak of 50,963 in 1973, but in 1978 was 48,309 – approximately one for every twenty adult communicants on the rolls. It would be hard to exaggerate the importance of this very large body of people who have made a public declaration of their faith and of their willingness to serve and who have been solemnly ordained to the service of Christ in the Church and in the nation. The fact that they accept a very considerable degree of responsibility means that they also have a considerable power. If they are diligent, they make up for many deficiencies in the ministry. They certainly relieve the ordained ministers from many tasks for which they have no taste nor training and so permit them to concentrate their energies on their own distinctive work. The impact made on industry, education, medicine and public life by such a large number of committed – mostly male – church members is very considerable and the contribution made by men of ability and experience to the life of the Church is beyond calculation.

The result of all this is that the Church of Scotland has retained its hold on the loyalty of the majority of the people of Scotland in a way which is not true of the Church of England, or the Churches in Wales or Ireland. This loyalty is sometimes shown in curious ways, even by those who do not attend its services. There is a story of a workman on Clydeside arguing against a proposal to have bishops in the Church. 'But', one of his mates objected, 'why should you bother? I thought you were an atheist.' 'So I am', was the reply, 'but I'm a Presbyterian atheist.'

To assess accurately the strength of the Church of Scotland as compared with other denominations is not always easy. Considerably more than one third of the population of Scotland has been baptized in the Church of Scotland. This is clear if one takes the total number of baptisms in relation to the number of children born. In 1921 there were 49,026 baptisms (123,201 children born); in 1941 34,627 (89,743 children born); in 1951 43,492 (90,635 children born); and in 1977 23,151 (62,244 children born). The proportion, it will be seen, has never fallen as low as one third and in one year, 1951, rose to almost one half. Curiously, the proportion in 1921 was just over a third, as it was in 1977. The figures supplied by the various church bodies are not a reliable way of assessing their relative strength. Some, for example, count all baptized persons; others all confirmed persons; and others only active members. Apart from the figures for baptisms, one objective way of arriving at an estimate is by taking the figures of denominational loyalty as given by patients in hospital. The chaplain of the largest hospital in Dundee made a random check recently. Some patients were too ill or confused to be asked and this, of course, increased the number of 'not known'. In addition, because of the large number of English people at the University, there was a higher proportion of Church of England members than would be found in other places. The proportion of Roman Catholics is always higher in the cities than in the burghs or rural areas. Here, however, are the figures:

Church of Scotland	414
Roman Catholic	116
Church of England	30
Episcopal	9
Other denominations	7
Not known	59

Allowing that some of the 'not known' are Church of Scotland, this would indicate that more than 66% of the patients can be regarded as belonging to that Church, at least in their own estimation.

Another objective way of assessing the strength of the various ecclesiastical bodies is by taking account of the figures of marriages as supplied by the Registrar General. In 1977 these were as follows:

Civil Marriages	14,270
Ecclesiastical Marriages	23,018 – made up as follows:
Church of Scotland	15,385
Other Presbyterian Churches	322
Roman Catholic	5,518
Episcopal	493
Others (Jews, Methodists, Baptists, Brethren)	1,300

From this it will be seen that marriages contracted in the Church of Scotland constitute 64% of all ecclesiastical marriages and 41% of all marriages.

Many of those who choose to be married in a Register Office would be Church of Scotland. The divorced, girls who are pregnant, elderly persons who 'do not want a fuss' and those marrying Roman Catholics and not wishing to go to either Church would fall into this category. In addition, a certain number of members of the Church of Scotland marrying Roman Catholics yield to the strong desire on the part of their prospective spouse to be married by a priest. These factors being allowed for, it is clear that in examining the present position and prospects of the Church of Scotland we are dealing with the 60%–70% of the population who would claim connection with that Church.

If one looks at the actual totals of adult communicant membership, however, the picture is not at first a very encouraging one. The total number of communicants rose in 1971 to a peak of 1,133,515. Since then it has fallen every year, although at a lessening rate. In 1978 it fell by 15,749 to 987,186. A drop of 146,000 in eight years seems disastrous, but when considering this apparent fall some factors must be borne in mind. For example, because congregations are increasingly assessed by Presbyteries for certain purposes on a per capita basis, there has recently been a tendency on the part of Kirk Sessions to adopt a fairly savage policy of pruning communion rolls, removing the names of any who are not really active. 13,944 were thus removed in 1978. Since this has been continuing for many years, there must by now be hundreds of thousands of communicants in the general population who are not on the rolls of congregations. Last year some 5,782 of these were readmitted as full communicant members, but a high proportion of the remainder would reckon themselves to be communicants, although no longer on any roll.

So much for crude totals of communicant membership. When one moves on to an analysis of these totals to take account of potential growth, the picture is more encouraging. The number of persons admitted on first profession of faith rose last year to 14,006, the second year in which there has been an increase. The number of baptisms also showed a slight increase, from 23,151 out of 62,244 children born, to 23,176 out of 62,300 children born – that is, from 34·6% to 34·8%.

In 1977, for the second year in succession, there was an increase in the numbers in Bible Classes (12–17 years) of over 2,000 from 28,246 to 30,342; of over 8,000 in the numbers in uniformed organizations from 128,575 to 136,937; in the numbers in youth clubs of 2,239 from 26,648 to 28,887; and in senior youth fellowships of 375 from 7,510 to 7,885. 1978 showed a drop in these figures, but even so, the figures for 1978 are higher than for 1976. There is therefore in every department of youth work save one evidence of growth. The sole exception is in the Sunday School, where numbers have been falling steadily from 210,890 in 1971 to 129,372 in 1978. There is perhaps no single cause to account for this. The fall in the birth rate is not in itself sufficient explanation. The increasing sophistication of educational methods in the day school must make the Sunday School with its shoe-string budget and its lack of facilities and educational aids seem dull to children. The lessening of parental authority has no doubt resulted in children going only to those church activities, such as youth fellowships or uniformed organizations, which appeal to them. One suspects that the drop is due largely to the falling away of the children of non-church parents. With television and the family car, the Sunday School no longer represents 'something to do' on Sunday or, what it once was, a way of getting rid of noisy children for an hour. With increasing wealth, the 'carrot' of the Christmas party or the annual outing no longer appeals. To some extent the drop in Sunday School scholars is compensated for by a con-

siderable improvement in the religious education given in schools
– particularly secondary schools. Sunday Schools apart, it would
appear that there are very definite signs of growth among young
people – teenagers and young parents – which is the very area in
which one would expect new growth first to be apparent.

Another very different but significant index of growth is the
Christian liberality of congregations. If people are not interested,
if, indeed, they do not attend church, they will not give. In the
year 1977 there was an increase of £1,863,717 (or 13·3%) in giving
by congregations. In 1978 there was a further spectacular increase
of £2,336,937 in congregational income. The actual income of
congregations has risen by more than £1,000,000 every year from
£7,659,815 in 1971 to £18,216,766 in 1978.

The encouraging statistics of youth work and of giving are all
the more satisfactory when account is taken of the widespread
social changes which might have been expected to militate against
church growth. Among such changes are the advent of radio and
television and the family car and the much greater mobility of the
population.

At a wedding in Glasgow some time ago the toast of the
bridesmaid was to have been proposed by a local Member of
Parliament. When he rose to speak, he said that before speaking
about the bridesmaid, he would give a brief address on the operation of the Rent Act, for, he said, 'I have turned up to give this
address on numerous occasions, only to find no audience to listen
to me. I do not intend to let this opportunity slip.' When he sat
down, he said that he had not been entirely jocular in his remarks,
for, he said, 'It is impossible to get an audience of any kind for a
political meeting between General Elections, not even always for a
Cabinet Minister.' As he asked, 'Why should people leave their
comfortable homes on cold nights to sit on hard benches in
draughty halls to hear someone speak whom they see on television
with the greatest regularity?' Television has killed other kinds of
public meetings too. Celebrity lectures are a thing of the past.
Philosophical, literary and debating societies have folded, cinemas
and theatres have shut down by the hundred. For the Church to
show even a slight growth is, therefore, all the more noteworthy.

One must compare its present position with what we might have expected to be its position or with the position of other bodies dependent on the gathering together of people in public places. Another disincentive to church growth which seems to have been well resisted is movements of population. One-third of the population of Scotland has been rehoused since the war, but that does not mean that the remaining two-thirds have remained in the houses they occupied in 1946. On the contrary, the centres of cities have been emptied of inhabitants, as have the rural areas, especially in the Borders and in the Highlands. The growth has been in new towns like Irvine, East Kilbride and Glenrothes, in the vast housing areas on the fringes of the cities and in dormitory towns within commuting distance of the cities.

The Church of Scotland has made valiant attempts to cope with this situation by closing down redundant churches in the once populous areas and by planting new churches where they are more needed. Since the reunion of the Churches in 1929, there have been 1,095 unions and 365 linkings. 240 new church buildings have been provided in new areas by the National Church Extension Movement initiated by the late Dr John White. Some of these new churches are now the largest and best attended in Scotland. In King's Park, Glasgow, for example, there are 1,777 communicants and in Netherlee – in the same Presbytery – 1,506. The building of new churches, however, can help only marginally with the problem of mobile population. The average length of stay of a family in a particular house has shrunk spectacularly. Many do not stay long enough in any place to put down roots and become connected with the parish church. Where people stayed for many years, baptisms, marriages, funerals or a stay in hospital afforded the minister an evangelical opportunity to involve those whom he was able to help in the work of the Church. Moreover, in a settled community, a minister was able to concentrate on new arrivals or on those with special needs. This is no longer possible. Even Paul would have found it hard to hold the attention of an audience on a moving staircase! The task is being tackled in Scotland by a constantly diminishing number of ministers, which makes the increases noted all the more remarkable. The reasons for the fall in the number of ministers – amounting to many hundreds – cannot be fully considered here. The fall in ministerial stipends relative to other professions is undoubtedly a factor. So also is the opening up of careers in social service to boys who at one time would have found an outlet for their desire to serve their fellows in the ministry. The fact that many wives have careers has added to the strain of what was once a joint enterprise by the minister and his wife. Other more subtle and complex causes may also be operative. Whatever the causes, the fact of the large reduction in the number of ministers makes it astonishing that the Church has continued to maintain its position.

In addition to those who appear in one way or another in church statistics, there is a very large 'hidden' Church in Scotland, as elsewhere, the strength of which cannot accurately be measured. This is constituted of those who come under the influence of the Word of God in one way or another without making any sort of public commitment. There has been a considerable development in recent years of chaplaincy service, for example, in schools, universities, industry, even in department stores and offices. At one time or another the present writer has taken services in an art school, in the office of a local government organization, in a school for the deaf, in a confectionery works, in an ancient grammar school, in a Territorial Army drill hall, for a Rotary Club, in a dockyard, in a Naval Club, in an infirmary. The extent of the impact made by these services is impossible to estimate, but the fact that they are asked for is not without significance. At least they release the Church from the Sunday ghetto and make clear that Christ is Lord of all life and not just Master of religion.

A second hidden Church is constituted of those who are exposed to religion on radio and television. One informed observer, the late Dr Ronald Falconer, took the view that this approached almost 100% of the population. Scottish Television has a 5-minute programme called 'Late Call' every night in the week in which ministers, priests and laymen and laywomen are given a fairly free hand. The number who watch it, especially among the unchurched, must be very great. Those who have appeared on it find that bus conductors, waitresses and ticket collectors hail them the next day with, 'Saw you on "Late Call" last night.' Other religious programmes of varying worth and value have a wide audience too. 'Stars on Sunday', 'Songs of Praise', 'Sunday Half Hour' may not include the most profound or challenging aspects of the faith, but all have some Christian content. The lectures given by the late Professor William Barclay had a profound impact on people of every social class, many of them allegedly unchurched.

So we come in the third place to take account of signs of life and adaptability which cannot be statistically measured. These are so numerous and so varied as to make it difficult to attempt any classification of them. No one of them of itself could be regarded as of major significance, but cumulatively they indicate a Church which is alive and growing. Celebrating the twenty-first anniversary of its first very limited beginning is St Ninian's, Crieff, a centre for the training of church members for the work of evangelism in parishes and in seaside missions. It can accommodate eighty. Also under the aegis of the Church of Scotland Home Board are two enterprises in the Highlands. The Compass Ski Club exists to promote the Christian Faith among those who find recreation in the mountains. It has premises at Glenshee Lodge, a residential centre for all the year round outdoor activities. The Warden of the Centre is a lay missionary. Badenoch Christian Centre, which opened in 1976, has given hospitality to about a thousand young people. Its aim is to bring as many young people as possible to faith in Christ. It combines Christian mission with the enjoyment of many outdoor activities. Established in 1962 by the gift of the Elphinstone family, the Carberry Tower Youth Leadership Training and Conference Centre has accommodation for 87 and aims primarily at providing courses for those working among young people. The Netherbow Centre for the Arts opened in September 1972, next door to John Knox's House in Edinburgh. It includes a theatre, a TV recording studio, a coffee house, a visual aids production unit and an art gallery. The centre contains within itself an ongoing debate between technology, the arts and ecology in the service of the gospel and gives expression to a belief in the wholeness of life in Christ.

Kirk Care is a very different venture from any of the foregoing.

It came into being at the end of 1973 out of a desire on the part of the Church's Committee on Social Service to diversify its care of the elderly through the provision of sheltered housing flats. The first two projects have been completed and over thirty others are at various stages of planning and erection. The social service undertaken by the Church of Scotland is extensive and constantly growing. There are twelve homes for children, forty-two for aged persons and twenty-eight for those with special needs – epileptics, alcoholics, young people in need of care, and the like. This department of the Church's work employs over a thousand persons.

The Church and Industry Committee of the Home Board has specified four areas of investigation – work to the glory of God, personal relationships, collective relationships and speaking the word. The Committee produces a bi-monthly news letter. The Industrial Mission of the Home Board is at work in ten major industrial areas, with full-time chaplains in four areas. The aim of the Mission is (a) to provide pastoral care and witness to the gospel for men and women in all branches of industry in their place of work; (b) to assess in the interest of the gospel the nature of the influence which industry exerts, both on individuals and on society; and (c) to promote the desire for just relationships and understanding at all levels of our industrial society. In 1970 a 'Society, Religion and Technology Project' was initiated. This continues, with a special emphasis on the problems of energy. Since the war, in addition to the Women's Guild with its 1,800 branches, some 670 Young Women's Groups have been formed.

The foregoing are but a selection of some of the projects and activities undertaken in recent years. Some would attach more importance to a few of these than to others, but the overall impression is of a Church with many growing points. The Moderator of the General Assembly visits four or five of the Presbyteries of the Church as well as all of the Universities, and is invited on various occasions to speak in every part of the country. Over the past few years each Moderator has commented in strikingly similar terms on the impressions left on him by these wide and varied contacts. Each has found evidence of 'a new hopefulness and a new enthusiasm, especially among young people' – to quote one of the Moderators' reports.

Such impressions are, of course, very subjective in character. There used to be a West Coast Mission in Scotland which ministered in some of the remoter areas of the Highlands and Islands. Once a year the missioners were required to fill up a schedule of details about their work. The last very daunting question on the schedule was, 'How many souls have been saved under your ministry in the past year?', to which one worthy man always gave the same answer, 'The Great Day will reveal it.' That, perhaps, is as much as one can ever say about any spiritual work. It is not required in stewards that they be successful, but only that they be faithful. It is but rarely, however, if we are faithful that the increase will be withheld from us. That would certainly be a safe deduction from the recent history and present position of Christ's Church in Scotland.

FOUR

Cathedrals and Growth
Centres of the spirit for the community

The Very Reverend ALAN WEBSTER,
Dean of St Paul's

The *Financial Times* for 18 October 1979 described the production of a 'musical theatre piece for performance in the Cathedral'. The report, under the heading 'Christian Fiesta', reviewed a resourceful production in Norwich Cathedral of John Paynter's 'The Voyage of St Brendan' which set the Cathedral ablaze with colour and movement. As the old Irish saint journeyed from his home through dangers from dragons, witches and icebergs, the audience-congregation – which included 500 children – and the actors felt drawn together by this parable of the human adventure. The packed Cathedral tingled to the sound of movement until finally the audience-congregation joined in Wesley's hymn 'Forth in thy Name, O Lord, I go'. Then, the reviewer tells us, 'scalps prickled and tears welled in the eyes. It was not altogether extravagant to say that this event went some way towards establishing a Cathedral Church as the centre of a community . . . even God himself could scarcely ask for more.'

Some years earlier, a poetry event entitled 'A Thousand Norfolk Poets' was staged in the same Cathedral. It involved both statutory and voluntary bodies as well as the cathedral clergy, the congregation and volunteer helpers. A special committee representing the education authority and the Chapter invited all the school children of the City of Norwich and the County of Norfolk to write a poem on any theme. More than a thousand children took part and the poems were mounted by volunteers on specially painted screens, set up round the nave of the Cathedral. Day after day hundreds of school children with their parents came to find their poems and to listen to poets, led by Ronald Blyth, Alan Brownjohn and Anthony Thwaite, read poems, comment on them and discuss the making of poetry. The floor of the nave was crowded with children of all ages listening to the poets talk and discuss the source of inspiration, the sense in which poetry comes from above and from outside. These young authors included some very sensitive and shrewd observers – it was noticeable how often poems from children living in Fenland areas, perhaps deprived of village and town community life, considered loneliness and suffering and old age. Certainly the co-operation of professional educationalists, volunteers and the paid staff of the Cathedral with the children and their parents, all generous with their time and talents, created an Event which revealed the spiritual resources of our community.

'Broadcasting stations for the voice of the poor', was how Albert van den Heuvel described the mission of cathedrals when speaking at the Deans and Provosts Conference at Coventry in 1966. 'Barchester Towers' is no more, and the staff of cathedrals have long since moved away from the kind of ministries described by Trollope, which buttressed the Church of England's reputation of being the Conservative Party at prayer. Cathedrals such as Manchester, Birmingham and Liverpool have all given outstanding service in the cause of racial integration, especially effective because it has been unobtrusive. The Dean of Liverpool reckons that he spends more than 50% of his time in this so-called 'secular work' – surely, however, it is spiritual and at the heart of the ministry to the community today. Canon John Collins, working from St Paul's, has built up one of the most powerful of the organizations which fight apartheid – 'Defence and Aid'. Several cathedrals have supported Richard Carr-Gomm of Abbeyfield fame in his concern for the needs of the lonely. The movement for the ordination of women, the concern for the humanization of prison policy, housing of exiles from Chile or Uganda, the work of Christian Aid, have all been backed by cathedrals. The visitor to a cathedral in Britain today is more likely to find evidence of this kind of concern than exhibitions about the problems of redundant churches, complex though these problems are.

The experience of work at Lincoln, Norwich and now St Paul's is that a new sophistication is expected of cathedrals. Whereas in the old days a small paid professional group, all men, usually ordained, apart from the organist and the chief administrator, settled the style and ministry, today the community is recognizing that cathedrals also belong to them. Of course, the need to provide finance for cathedrals has always drawn men and women of goodwill. Today the actual ministry is carried on in cathedrals by Christians with many shades of personal conviction – Roman Catholics, who wish Mass was still in Latin; liberals whose faith is fed by Hans Küng; radical theologians and fundamentalists who long to see Billy Graham preaching in every cathedral in Britain. St Albans has filled its great nave with a gathering of artists entitled 'The Hands of the Craftsmen'. Many cathedrals have created festival banners, amongst the most splendid being those at Winchester, Southwark and Truro. Their sheer spaciousness, as well as the tradition of artistic tolerance, gives those who minister in cathedrals a challenging opportunity.

Goodwill leaps the national and denominational barriers. St Giles', Edinburgh, sends its Minister to the Deans and Provosts Conference, at which Westminster Cathedral also has an observer. When the 600th anniversary of the *Revelations of Divine Love* of Julian of Norwich was celebrated on 8 May 1973, admirers of Julian came from America, France and Italy. A Jesuit lectured, a Methodist poet wrote new hymns; bishops and chairmen – Anglican, Roman Catholic, Free Church – attended an ecumenical Eucharist. When the rose petals, pink in the clear East Anglian sunlight, drifted down from the high windows of the Norman nave at the final blessing, some of the nuns from England and France caught the petals and put them in their missals as if to carry away the memory. We were given hazel nuts from Norwich Market to remind us of one of Julian's most powerful images. Afterwards, with the Julian themes of 'see and trust' and 'be silent' in our minds, we processed through the streets to the site of the Anchorite's cell. The memory of that service, a glimpse of heavenly unity, is more powerful than those faint-hearted denominational divisions which still impede the spirit of love.

All these events depend on trust and co-operation beyond the usual structures. Most Anglican cathedrals are governed by statutes, rather meagrely revised in 1963, which, for instance, make it difficult for women or members of other churches to be members of cathedral staffs – though there are now some deaconesses giving a new dimension to work and thinking at some of the cathedrals. Ecumenism seems to be growing in power, though in 1977 no Free Churchman or Roman Catholic took a vocal part in the National Jubilee Service in St Paul's. However, at the official services for the Order of the British Empire at St Paul's, it is now the custom for the service to be shared by ministers of different Churches. There is ground-level ecumenism in cathedrals amongst communicants. At St Paul's, I notice how many Roman Catholics from the continent make their communion every Sunday. Though primates and patriarchs find it hard to agree, at the ordinary level of Christian worship there is a loving tolerance which will eventually change the structure and substitute trust and co-operation for always looking at the rules and resolving 'Better not'.

Time for meditation and leisure for reflection is so precious and so easily destroyed that those who minister at cathedrals struggle hard to make room for the Spirit to work at these deep levels. I have experienced Wells in the dusk of a summer evening, kept open by volunteer vergers. At St John the Divine in New York, each week a different parish group spends twelve hours, starting at 8 p.m. in the evening, with supper and baseball in the crypt, then Eucharist and a silent watch above in the vast unfinished shrine on Cathedral Heights, Manhattan. You cannot forget the Minster at Lincoln, where by long established tradition, students in training for ordination spend part of Maundy Thursday evening in silence. The Angel Choir at Lincoln, lit by moonlight and one or two tiny bulbs, is unforgettable for all those who trained at the theological college on that hill above the city and spent those hours together, with Gethsemane at the back of their minds. The British Council of Churches showed imagination and courage at its Liverpool Youth Conference when most events took place in Liverpool Cathedral during the hours of darkness. There are many problems about opening huge cathedrals at night but the idea of some night

occasions each year is spreading. How commendable was the
courage of the staff of Notre Dame in Paris, when they allowed the
thousands of students at the 1979 Taizé Festival to continue far into
the evening, the whole cathedral full of young people.

To make the gospel intelligible has always been the primary task
of preachers. Congregations are increasing at most cathedrals at the
main morning service, and now at St Paul's are rarely less than a
thousand. The task of preaching the gospel in such a way as to
communicate with the outsider or the person who is half interested
is crucial. Only on television, the radio and the rest of the media
are there such opportunities for speaking across the frontier which
often divides the normal workaday world from the ecclesiastical.
There have been cathedrals which, in practice, have been castles of
conservative clericalism. Now the number of seekers for faith who
come to cathedrals has changed our agenda. My own experience,
successively at Lincoln, Norwich and St Paul's, has convinced me
that cathedrals need theologians on their staff and theologians need
the opportunities which cathedrals can give, particularly those of
listening and teaching within a worshipping community which is
open to the uncommitted visitor. Theologians who attempt the
task of interpreting Christianity and making the gospel intelligible
to the questioning enquirer, receive an immense welcome as
preachers and teachers. It is no accident that Bishop John Robin-
son, Dr Hans Küng, Fr Harry Williams and other theologians who
attempt to answer the questions people actually ask achieve such
astonishing sales of their work. Conversations and consultations
with cathedral worshippers show that there are many who in fact
question the infallibility of the Pope and the Church yet believe in
Jesus Christ, while remaining agnostic about the precise details of
his birth or the exact nature of his resurrection body. Again the
traditions of spaciousness and tolerance within cathedrals provides
a foil where men, women and young children can be helped to
find their own way to an honest faith – not least those who wish to
remain both honest scientists and honest believers.

Christian worship both attracts and repels such enquirers. In the
texts of liturgies, creeds, hymns, anthems and prayers, there are
often phrases which are best understood as symbols, poetry, myths,

rather than as literal historical or dogmatic claims. It is a mistake to try to rewrite many of these texts. It is wisest to supply explanatory prefaces where the different approaches to the great themes of God can be explored. I have been fortunate at St Paul's to receive the thoughtful co-operation of a liberal Jewish Rabbi in preparing a preface for the Advent Carol Service which discussed the profound theme of waiting for the Messiah. At times, prayers ought to be changed. In Christmas Carol Services a prayer is sometimes used which suggests that we are praying for 'sinners', as if we were not included among them. Now that there is a general understanding of the psychological teaching of Freud and Jung and of the theological teaching that in his service only wounded soldiers can serve, it is important that prayers should be so phrased that our own awareness of ourselves includes an awareness of our own sinfulness. The more intercessions at the Eucharist can use the minds and voices of men *and women* who have experienced exile, imprisonment and deep personal suffering, the more these prayers can open us to the divine grace. I shall not forget the Cathedral Christmas Eucharist, when the Lord's Prayer was led in Spanish by refugees from the Marxists who had been driven from their homes in Chile. The crowded county and city congregation felt, as they heard those voices coming over the loudspeakers, that they really were at one with those for whom there was no room at the inn, those who had travelled many thousands of miles to find a tolerant freedom. Even at a Christmas Eucharist, the Cross should be in our prayers. The task of interpretation and making intelligible for us today requires the use of many minds and many voices. I hope that the time will come when the theologians will provide prefaces for the great moments of worship, when the cathedrals and the churches are crowded – Advent Carols, Christmas Carols, Easter Services, Community Festival Services and Harvest Thanksgiving.

The preface to the Advent Carol Service to which I have referred read thus:

Advent means waiting for the coming of God. How often we wait. People are waiting in Zimbabwe-Rhodesia not knowing what the next year will bring. People are waiting in Gulag Archipelago hoping for the years to pass and release to be proclaimed. People are waiting in areas where there is racial tension, anxious about the next demonstration. Sometimes we wait in fear, sometimes in hope. People wait for the birth of a baby, for an examination result, for news of an operation, for a meeting with someone greatly loved. Humanity has always been waiting for better times, for justice, for peace.

Advent Services are designed to strengthen our discipline so that, as we wait with the rest of humanity, we do so specially to detect God at work, often in quiet, unambitious projects. Advent looks to the present and to the future. Our faith hints that it will be a birth, not a catastrophe.

The Old Testament tells how the Jews learned to wait for deliverance from slavery in Egypt. In the morning watch, Exodus records, the Lord discomfited their enemies. Centuries later, they learned to wait on God till he should deliver them from captivity in Babylon. They began to look forward to a new age of prosperity, peace and joy – to be brought in by one whom God would appoint and send – the Messiah. And still, the Jews are waiting, some wishing to hurry on the Messiah, some sure that mankind is not yet ready, but all waiting in confidence that God is with them.

In our day, men and women return again and again to the theme of waiting. *Waiting for Godot* is a modern morality play on this theme. Poets insist that we miss the signals and do not hear each other. Stevie Smith writes, 'I was much further out than you thought and not waving but drowning.' Simone Weil sees 'attention à Dieu' as the heart of religion, the one absolute. R. S. Thomas observes, in *Laboratories of the Spirit*, 'In cities that have outgrown their promise, people are becoming pilgrims . . . you must remain kneeling . . . prayer too has its phases . . . As I have always known, he would come unannounced.'

When Jesus came, many believed that he was the one humanity had always been waiting for: and Christians the world over can never believe otherwise. This service revives the old longings and affirms our expectations. We pray that God will lighten our darkness and the darkness of this world.

We watch the Choir moving slowly forward, making our own their urgent petition,

> May Christ's peace come!
> May Christ's kingdom come!

At the end we pray together, asking that we may be disciplined and alert, trusting in God who comes to his people, to every human being.

The music, details of which are given with the words of each hymn and carol and anthem, is drawn from all ages of the Church's history. We see in particular how composers from every tradition have been inspired to adapt and enrich old melodies and to bring new life to traditional words by music of their own.

Cathedrals are pilgrimage centres. The British Tourist Authority reckons that eighteen million people visit English cathedrals every year. We suggest that the traffic is increasingly becoming two-way. Clergy, and members of Winchester Cathedral choir celebrated its 900th centenary by a tour in North America. Young people from many cathedrals, especially where there are Young Friends, share in many pilgrimages; close at hand to Coventry or Iona, further afield to Taizé or L'Arche in France, further still to the Focolare Centre in Italy and further still, to the countries of the Third World. The French movement Accueil Rencontre Communauté, pioneered by Professor Jean-Pierre Bagot from Paris and Père Aye from Boulogne, has done much to interpret ecumenical pilgrimage between English and French cathedrals. It aims to transform a visit to a building into an experience of cathedrals of the spirit — communities of many nations feeling a common membership of God's human families, so that pilgrimage at its deepest level is reborn.

It is easy to dismiss modern tourism as simply commercial, or to comment with a groan that every teenager today is his own Marco Polo. Perhaps in God's eyes, nothing matters more than that we should understand cultures other than our own and, coming from the rich world, appreciate the real needs of the Third World. From these journeys we may

> Learn who and where and how we are
> The children of a modest star. . . .
> How hard to stretch imagination
> To live according to our station
> (W. H. Auden,
> *Collected Longer Poems* (Faber 1968), p. 90)

The deepening of pilgrimage is an essential role for ministry at cathedrals today. It is not enough to send a choir or an orchestra as a group of professional musicians, though that is better than nothing. What is needed is the conscious effort to understand, to listen and to bring back a fresh appreciation of life in Calcutta, or Zimbabwe or New York. It will be better still when nationals of other countries can live at other cathedrals and welcome their own compatriots. When our four French visitors, led by Professor Jean-Pierre Bagot, spent the month of July 1979 at St Paul's, as others were doing at Canterbury and elsewhere, the spark of the spirit seemed to leap again and again and enable casual visitors from France to be transformed into pilgrims. The hosts in a German home in Westphalia to a mother and her chorister son at one cathedral felt so bound in friendship and concern that when, three years later, the chorister was tragically killed in a road accident, the two German hosts, though speaking almost no English, travelled to Norwich for the boy's funeral.

However many welcomers there are at cathedrals, it will never be possible to give a personal greeting to the huge crowds that come, especially in the summer. Here, growing points in ministry are the exhibitions designed to interpret the understanding of the gospel to the visitor, as at Canterbury, Durham, Norwich and elsewhere. Here, once again, cathedrals are building on an ancient tradition. The Centre Pompidou in Paris, probably the most successful interpretative centre in Europe, explicitly borrows from medieval cathedrals the idea of a large piazza in front, so that the visitor passes through activity, both spontaneous and organized, before he reaches the entrance forum, itself an idea linked to those basilicas which were the parents of our cathedrals. To spend a few days in the Centre Pompidou or in the Museum of London or in the more adventurous American Visitors' Centres, shows what can be done to interpret ideas for the visitor, whether he has half an hour or half a day.

The staffs of cathedrals have found the setting up of these interpretative exhibitions exhilarating. If we learn best by teaching, my experience of working for two or three years with committees on the theme of cathedral exhibitions, has been amongst the most challenging tasks of my ministry. I remember the young exhibition designer saying, 'You are asking me to exhibit God but he is invisible.' I remember the day-long discussion between those who wished the explanation of the gospel to be primarily historical and those who pressed that philosophical questions must be faced. Ought an exhibition in a cathedral to indicate that in many parts of a Christian country it appears that 'God is dead', judging by the housing and conditions of life often imposed upon people young and old? 'Let us call this exhibition The Vision of God.' 'No, that will be felt exclusive by those who are simply conscious of a vacuum in their life and cannot yet make a positive commitment.' 'Let us then call it both: The Vision of God – a Search for Meaning', and so it was decided. I shall not forget the young artist reading *The Revelations of Divine Love* by Julian of Norwich for the first time, and painting with strong realism the Vision of the Hazelnut.

The goodwill towards cathedrals if they will try to explain what they stand for and interpret the spiritual dimension is enormous. I remember going to the Corning Glass Visitors' Centre in New York State and spending a day with the Directors discussing the necessity of honesty in exhibitions. They insisted that just as a multinational corporation such as Corning Glass must exhibit its dangers and failures, so an honest cathedral exhibition must acknowledge that Darwin, Marx and Freud had some justification for their agnostic attitude towards the institution of the Church. I remember the goodwill of many leading photographers, not least the willingness of Lord Snowdon to contribute some of his most powerful studies of the life of neglected children. Film technicians, visual aid artists, museum directors, newspapermen, experts in tourism have all given their time and skill to the slow process of planning which must precede the final documentation which can be handed to the professional designers. To stand at a cathedral exhibition, at the section designed by a group of scientists, which suggests that the universe is complex at the microscopic level, is to experience witness. 'Do you mean that you clergy realize how hard it is to be an honest scientist and an honest believer?' 'Yes, that is why this section of this exhibition has been placed here, not to argue you into belief but to deepen your questioning, to show clearly that members of churches have their problems and questions and have to grow in understanding and faith.'

If churches are to respond to the community's anxiety about its spiritual vacuum, then churches must listen to the community around them and welcome the community in their activities. Churches can become cliques. Many find that they cannot join any of the churches. The secular culture is more open to the religious impulse than ever before since the rise of science. The Christmas story, especially, with its mystery and poetry, is a powerful myth which moves minds and wills. God as Spirit is experienced by many who are not church members. Churches, chapels, cathedrals, find that the community allows, even expects them, to take a lead. Cathedrals are no longer dinosaurs left over by the demise of Christendom but can be community centres for the spirit.

No doubt the many mistakes made by religious bodies in their long history are remembered against them. But certainly they are felt, especially at Easter and Christmas and other festivals, to have been faithful to the gospel. My experience is that, when they are open to enquirers and try to make the gospel intelligible, then they begin to grow. Many churches, chapels and cathedrals found themselves packed for Carol Services. St Paul's in 1979 had to shut the doors for safety, excluding hundreds of worshippers. They had come for an hour or so to focus on the hopes and faith of the community around them. The fact that the community is pluralist, complex and sophisticated does not impede the ministry of cathedrals, so long as those who arrange their worship are sensitive to the varied needs of the worshippers.

Today a new Reformation is slowly changing the structures of the Church. As fewer men are ordained each year (only 99 men in 1977 for the whole of France), so the traditional parochial system of one professional priest full time in every parish is being eroded. Now the voluntary help from men *and women* is needed to enable the churches to be the spiritual centres of community. The house churches and other small groups who discuss philosophical, religious and ethical issues and whch cluster round cathedrals and parish churches are showing in practice the way the Spirit is leading us. I have experienced very informal celebrations of the

Holy Communion, often Series 3 but not always, in private houses, cathedral staff houses or conference houses. These celebrations add a dimension to the crowded occasions in large buildings. They also train men and women and younger people to lead worship acceptably and without embarrassment. Simply to amalgamate more and more parishes under a single clergyman to meet the problem of the shortage of vocations, leads, as one layman put it recently, 'to a third-rate job all round. In this village, we sometimes have a lady lay preacher and she is splendid, but of course, restricted in her duties.' Similarly, there is a slow acceptance in the large staffs of cathedrals of the qualities which can be given by a well-trained deaconess who can do much pastoral, liturgical and educational work which needs the full-time thought and expertise of a member of the staff.

Where the Church is listening to lay people and is aware of the discontent with the materialistic life which seems to engulf us, then ways are found of breaking through the ecclesiastical barriers which seem to separate the institutional Church from so much workaday life. The wife of one of my friends is an industrial chaplain. She is spending three months on a factory shift which packs fish fingers. The work is boring, noisy, smelly and often very impersonal but the women with whom she works are warm, open and very accepting. Five of them came to her licensing and had all their preconceptions about the Church knocked out of them. They thought that the Church would be cold, that the walls would be grey stone and bare and that the people would be 'stuck up'. They were wrong in each case. Again, at cathedrals where there are volunteer guides who go out of their way to welcome, shake hands, offer to help in every way, then people are surprised and learn that the Church has an accepting human face. Personal greetings given by men and women in cathedrals, cups of coffee together after services, taking trouble to listen to what people want and know their names, give a new personal dimension to worship.

My experience of cathedrals during the last twenty years, first at Lincoln, then at Norwich, and now at St Paul's, is of increasing commitment to interpretation by the staff, the worshippers, the musicians – everyone concerned with cathedrals. There used to be a time when cathedrals seemed almost not to be part of the Church, let alone aware of the need to make the Christian faith intelligible, to let the gospel speak to our contemporary society, particularly in the centre of cities. 'Go away, we are going to have a service' is the caricature of some attitudes in the past. Now, I suppose the most common remark is, 'Welcome to your Cathedral. How can we help you?' No doubt, the question is often, 'Tell me the way to the crypt . . . or the toilets . . . or the Whispering Gallery', but these questions, if they can be answered and the conversation continued, will lead to companionship on the pilgrimage. What so many come seeking in cathedrals is experience – worship or music or a conversation which speaks to them. Cathedrals are growing because this experience is a reality.

FIVE

Signs of Growth
On looking back

The Reverend Dr F. W. DILLISTONE,
formerly Dean of Liverpool

I

The image of growth has become one of the most popular of our time. Particularly in the world of economics we look anxiously for signs of growth in productivity; if it falls below a certain percentage, the alarm bells begin to ring; if it approaches zero it is assumed that we are heading for disaster. Growth is measured by surveys, statistics, numbers, calculations, just as the growth of the human body can be measured in terms of height and weight.

Similar statistical measurements are used in the worlds of education, of health and of social welfare. It is not therefore surprising that over the past fifty years they have also been employed increasingly in the affairs of the Church. Numbers of baptisms, confirmations, church weddings, candidates for the ministry, are recorded annually and comparisons are then made. Clergy stipends, responses to financial appeals, voluntary contributions, quotas for central funds are constantly under surveillance. All too easily it comes to be imagined that these are the all-important matters when coming to some judgement about what constitutes growth or decline.

But are those the most significant criteria? If so, there is little that I can report from a backward look for I have no reliable figures available by which to compare the numerical state of affairs as it existed in the Church of England in the 1920s with that which exists today. On the other hand, he would be a bold man who tried to assess what was the inward *spiritual* state of, shall we say, the majority of church members in the earlier period and then pro-

ceeded to claim that it was deeper or richer or more commendable
than that of a similar cross-section in the Church today. Appeals
can obviously be made to what are called 'facts and figures' on the
one side and to signs of spiritual fervour on the other but there are
surely other criteria by which growth or decline can be observed
and evaluated.

II

Growth is an essential property of *life*. 'Growth', John Henry
Newman wrote, 'is the only evidence of life.' This assertion may
be too sweeping but it is certainly in the *life* of a child or of an
animal or of a tree that we look for evidence of growth. Yet it is
not sufficient simply to watch for growth in height or bulk: there
can, alas, be deformities and even cancerous growths within a
living organism. Moreover life cannot be confined to physical
developments. The child who truly lives grows in knowledge of
the world and of society, in powers of discrimination between the
valuable and the worthless, in abilities for self-expression and for
the achievement of desired ends.

We can, I think, only talk about the growth of a society or an institution in so far as we use this model of a growing individual. As I
have suggested, in this model there is a place for quantitative and
measurable features but those seem to me to be the least important.
I shall be concerned rather with growth in understanding, in
expression, in proportion, in the framing and implementation of
policies. What evidences of growth can be discerned by looking
back over the period since the First World War?

The first that I want to emphasize is growth in the *field of
ecumenical contacts and relationships*. The end of the nineteenth
century saw the denial of the validity of Anglican orders by Papal
decree: the early years of the twentieth century witnessed strong
antagonisms between Anglicans and members of the Free
Churches, particularly in relation to denominational schools; the
First World War cut off the Churches in England from the great
Lutheran and Reformed Churches on the Continent. There was
the danger that the Church of England would turn in upon itself,

spending its time in seeking to justify its own existence as an authentic member of the divinely constituted and continuously preserved catholic Church of Christ and failing to grow by relating itself to its wider environment in the way in which every organism must do if it is to remain healthy.

It is well known that there was much hesitancy in the Church of England about appointing official representatives to be present either at the great International Missionary Conference in Edinburgh in 1910 or at the first Conference on Faith and Order in Lausanne in 1926. Yet by the time of the Jerusalem Missionary Conference in 1928, leading Anglicans such as William Temple and Charles Raven were entering fully into the concern for greater co-operation between the non-Roman Churches in the task of world-evangelization, while at the Edinburgh Conference on Faith and Order in 1937 one of the most notable contributions to the concern for eucharistic understanding amongst the participants was made by Bishop F. C. N. Hicks who would have been generally regarded as belonging to the more 'catholic' wing of the Church of England.

Again, in the area of worship, there was not only the obvious stretching out to the works of the great liturgical scholars such as Duchesne and Jungmann and to influential writers on the spiritual life such as Baron von Hügel and Henri Brémond, all members of the Roman Catholic Church, but also to the Swedish Lutheran, Yngve Brilioth (whose book *Eucharistic Faith and Practice* opened new doors to ecumenical understanding), and to the German Lutherans, Rudolf Otto and Friedrich Heiler, whose books on the experience of the Holy and on the manifold forms of prayer in human experience gained a wide readership in England in the period between the Wars.

Thus there was a slow but steady growth in readiness to co-operate in mission and to learn from other traditions in worship. There can be little doubt that much of this new outgoingness was the result of friendships made and understanding gained in student circles. One of the most remarkable features of the religious life of England in the first half of the twentieth century was the drawing together, in Christian fellowship and witness, of students

belonging to different denominations but finding a deep unity in
prayer and service. In college groups and summer conferences
personal relationships were established which helped men and
women to continue growing towards a more comprehensive unity
when the time came for them to occupy positions of responsibility
in their several Churches.

I had the privilege of being a delegate to the Assembly of the
World Council of Churches held at New Delhi in 1961. The great
conference tent was the site of the united service of worship on the
first Sunday morning, the form of which was the eucharistic rite of
the (Anglican) Church of India, Burma and Ceylon. Not all of
those present felt able to participate to the extent of receiving the
bread and the wine but the majority did so, the invitation being
given to all communicant members of the more than 100 churches
there represented. Just over fifty years had passed since 1910.
Growth within the Church of England? That a branch of the
Anglican Communion acted as host, that the Archbishop of
Canterbury was present as one of the Presidents of the World
Council of Churches, were striking evidences of the way in which
the Church of England, which in the 1920s was still in many
respects insular and held within the traditional boundaries,
whether of a national or ecclesiastical kind, had grown into a body
able to play its full part in the international and ecumenical
Christian fellowship.

What had by 1961 become an accepted aspect of its life in
relation to the Protestant and Reformed Churches, has, since
Vatican II in 1962, become increasingly evident also in relation to
the Roman Catholic Church. So far the change has not been
characterized by formal associations such as have been established
through the British Council of Churches and the World Council
of Churches or the great interdenominational federations of
students. But in innumerable ways the atmosphere has changed,
making possible a vast increase in personal contacts and inter-
communications which are the indispensable preliminaries
to deeper understanding and growth in mutual confidence
and trust. Growth takes place in any organism as its receptors draw
in appropriate nutrients from the environment. More formal

bonds of inter-relationship may in time be created. For the time being, the growth towards friendship and better understanding over the past twenty years has been, in my judgement, one of the most encouraging features of the English scene.

III

The second area where, as it seems to me, there have been marked evidences of growth is that of truly *corporate worship*. I look back to the 1920s. Three patterns of public worship could be clearly distinguished in the Church of England. In many parishes, probably the majority, the forms authorized by the Prayer Book were faithfully observed with a relatively small number of worshippers present at the early service of Holy Communion, larger numbers either at Mattins or at Evensong. Active congregational participation was largely confined to a few prescribed prayers and to the singing of hymns, the clergy and choir being responsible for the rest. There was little concern for innovation. Services were performed decently and when choirs were well trained, with musical excellence. Preaching tended towards the stressing of moral duties and virtues — the maintenance of the traditional standards of religious and ethical propriety.

But there were also churches commonly designated as High or Low, Anglo-Catholic or Evangelical. In the former the central service on Sunday was the Sung Eucharist or High Mass. Much care and attention was given to details of ritual: the sermon could often be a powerful advocacy of Catholic doctrine. The priest represented the congregation in offering the symbolic sacrifice and this was held to constitute the essence of Christian worship. Church buildings were adapted or freshly designed to enable attention to be focused upon the high altar, which was set in the area where the most solemn rites of the eucharistic drama were performed. In this drama there were minor functionaries; the larger congregation responded in prayers, hymns and ritual acts.

In Low and Evangelical Churches there was a strong emphasis upon a minimum of ritual objects and actions. The east end of the church was usually plain and unadorned and there was strict adherence to the liturgical form authorized in the Book of Common Prayer. The chief focus of attention for the congregation was the Bible, read in the lessons and expounded through preaching. The task of the minister was pre-eminently that of interpreting the Bible's directions for faith and conduct; the congregation was called upon to listen diligently and to follow these directions in actual practice.

To describe the situation in this way is to be guilty of over-simplification and generalization. There were variations and gradings and combinations but the polarization between High and Low was marked while between the two it was easy to be content with a regular routine of prescribed forms and ceremonies. Attempts to gain authorization for revised or alternative forms were defeated through the decision of Parliament in 1928, and in England little was heard of the Liturgical Movement during the 1930s. But I think it can be claimed that from about 1940 onwards new signs of growth began to appear within the worship forms and activities of the Church of England. A way began to appear by which new forms of worship could gain united acceptance by large numbers who had hitherto struggled to preserve and further their own limited and distinctive traditions.

A tree makes steady growth both by extending its roots deeper into the ground, drawing upon resources of water and chemical substances, and also by stretching out its branches and leaves to suck in nutrients from the environment. A notable book, *The Shape of the Liturgy*, by the Anglican scholar Dom Gregory Dix, looked back at the central actions which characterized the eucharistic liturgy in the earliest period of the Church's life: church buildings, church furnishings, the words and actions of ministers and layfolk all served to re-present the series of dramatic actions as instituted by Christ himself. Then in relation to the contemporary environment the book, *Liturgy and Society*, by another Anglican scholar, A. G. Hebert, focused attention upon the way in which the varying aspects of the Eucharist, and in particular the communion of the people, could be related to the needs of the social order as they were becoming apparent in the twentieth-century world.

Gradually those who had tried to isolate and defend a particular form of worship in the Church became aware of new possibilities of uniting by rediscovering the characteristic forms of early Christian worship and by using forms of language and ritual activities relevant to society today. In architecture, forms which had already been pioneered on the Continent began to appear in English churches, forms designed to make it possible for the president at the Eucharist to gather the people around him and for the people on their part to gain a heightened sense of true participation in the eucharistic actions. New forms of ritual action began to be designed to allow maximum participation by the laity in reading the lections, leading the prayers, offering the gifts of bread and wine and sharing the peace. Finally experimental language-forms were permitted in which the traditional and the contemporary could be joined, it was hoped, in fruitful interchange.

The past thirty years have seen many changes and developments in corporate worship within the Church of England. Have the manifestations of the Liturgical Movement been signs of growth or evidences of decline from the honoured traditions of Anglican practice and the classical language of the Book of Common Prayer? Judgements will differ amongst those who debate this question. I can only express my own conviction that no single development in the Church of England has done more to promote tolerance and respect and fellowship amongst those with different backgrounds of training and experience than the wide acceptance of a truly congregational celebration of the Eucharist around the Lord's table, using new forms of language and ritual expression.

I well remember the formalities and, I am bound to say, unrealities of Sunday Evensong in College Chapel in my undergraduate days, an exercise in which all members of the College were expected to engage six times a term unless exempted for some very good reason. In contrast, nearly sixty years later, I shared in a Sunday evening Eucharist in the Chapel of another College in Oxford. For me it was a joyful and moving experience. One could not but feel that all who were present (a very good attendance now including women with men) were actively involved, sharing in responsive words and in the leadership of intercessions, playing their parts in the symbolic actions which belong to the eucharistic movement. And this was no isolated event. I cannot but believe that there has been significant growth within the Church at least within this area of its life. Worshipping activities, even of relatively small groups, can promote the health of the whole body. Some at least of the old divisive interpretations and ritual actions have been transcended, making possible a new sense of growing together within the Body of Christ.

IV

As soon as we attempt to consider the relation of the Church to its wider environment we find ourselves on much more debatable ground. Over the past half century, our knowledge of and manipulation of the natural order have advanced by leaps and bounds, while such major upheavals have taken place in the social order that it becomes difficult in the extreme to assess what the effects of all this has been upon the Church itself. Has it failed to relate itself to these new dynamic conditions? Inevitably its members live in the contemporary world and cannot fail to be influenced by it in innumerable ways. By the very fact that it inherits so long and so impressive a tradition, the Church cannot avoid being conservative on many issues. Has conservatism so prevailed that the Church has lagged behind and made no growth in its understanding of and influence upon the changing structures? The world scene is so complex that no simple answer can be given to such a question. I can only give a few personal impressions while others may well have different ideas.

The field of *Communication*. In this we are all playing our parts daily. On the one hand we talk, make signals, write, type, convey information; on the other hand we listen, observe, read, decode. This is a constant process. As long as a community remains relatively small and relatively stable, its communications-system presents no major difficulties though it is always possible to misunderstand and misinterpret individual messages. When, however, communities are situated in areas characterized by widely varying physical conditions and widely divergent cultural histories, or when one community advances into a new apprehension of world order and social change while a contiguous neighbouring community clings strenuously to the past, communications gaps grow wider and wider. There is no common growth and the slower of the two tends to be counted out.

Presumably the most obvious example of rapid development in this century has been that of scientific knowledge and technological achievement. This development has been accompanied by, and in many respects made possible by, a vast proliferation of new technical terms or by the use of existing words and symbols in new ways. This is true in business, in industry, in medicine, in education. It becomes increasingly difficult for one who is not actively involved in some particular discipline — a scientific department, a service industry, a technical enterprise — to speak its language and to understand its operations. Can the Church ignore all that is in process in the burgeoning world of science and technology? Can it confine its concerns to the *leisure* and *domestic* activities of mankind? Can it rest content with language-forms which are connected with family relationships or the common experiences in the natural order — the sun, the earth, the wind, the fire — or with common attitudes in the social order — love, hate, care, hostility — but make no attempt to grasp the larger and more complex patterns of physical and social relations which have become so dominant a concern in this century? If God is concerned with the total cosmos and with the whole range of human existence, must not the Church seek to relate itself likewise to the totality of the order within which it finds itself and to identify itself with God's purpose for its salvation and sanctification?

This is an immensely difficult problem and the ordinary church member can hardly be blamed for deciding to stay with familiar forms relating to his own more immediate concerns and to leave the bigger questions to the experts. The danger of this is that a major part of his daily life may seem to have no connection with his religion. The language of faith is confined to a limited area; the wider world goes on its way unconcerned and unchallenged about moral and personal issues.

It is not perhaps surprising that *natural* theology, which has traditionally been related to the whole cosmic order, has passed through a difficult period in this century. The great classical philosophers were very much concerned with the creation and preservation and goal of the universe, and theologians of the Church of England regarded these philosophers as a valid source of enlightenment and guidance leading on to the revealed writings of Holy Scripture. Even up until the 1920s Anglican theologians could write freely about the connections between creation and incarnation, between nature and grace; the notion of a divine Creator and the categories of form and substance and cause still remained dominant. The universe could be regarded, in its totality, as a partial revelation of God's design and will and purpose: the incarnation was not an isolated event but rather the particular and climactic revelation within his total creative activity.

Approximately half a century ago three Anglican theologians tried to come to terms with the new concepts of emergent evolution and creative process and to relate them to earlier forms of natural theology. C. E. Raven in *Creator Spirit*, L. S. Thornton in *The Incarnate Lord* and William Temple in *Nature, Man and God*, each in his own way sought to present a natural theology which could find its fulfilment in the Christian revelation of God, Father, Son and Holy Spirit. But the long period during which classical philosophy had undergirded Christian theology was almost at an end. The upsurge of analytical and linguistic and empirical philosophy meant that Christian theologians must look in other directions for paradigms and language-forms to interpret the natural order theistically. And this was a task of no mean complexity.

Only a few in the past thirty years have felt equipped to undertake the task of stretching out towards the scientific theories and technological constructions of our contemporary world, maintaining a dialogue with them and reformulating aspects of Christian theology as a result. Yet it seems clear that this is an essential strategy for growth. It does not mean at all that positivistic or deterministic outlooks must be swallowed, however popular they may be in some quarters. But if the world is God's world, then the new methods being used by scientists and technologists to understand that world and to utilize its resources need surely to be learned by Christians, at least in some measure, in order that they may make judgements concerning the successes and the limitations of these methods. Valuable contributions have been made by Anglican scholars such as E. L. Mascall, Ian Ramsey, John Habgood and Arthur Peacocke but much remains to be done, especially in communicating contributions of this kind to those who have to live and move, day by day, in environments which are now so largely structured by technological inventions.

V

A second challenge to the natural theologian has come through the expansion, during the period with which I am concerned, of both general and specialized knowledge of the world's non-Christian religions. Up until the Second World War this knowledge had been largely confined to a small number of university scholars and to missionaries who learned about these religions on the field. But the vast increase in the mobility of peoples as a result of wars, air travel and immigration, coupled with the new and vivid means of observation provided by the camera and television, has meant that today far more people in England have some knowledge of Islam, Hinduism and Buddhism than has ever been the case before. How are they to relate this knowledge to traditional Christian values? Can their own faith be deepened and strengthened through new encounters and can they therefore *grow* thereby?

At the Jerusalem Conference of the International Missionary Council in 1928 it was widely felt that the influence of the ancient religions was waning. As literacy spread and as men became aware of the achievements of modern secular civilization, would there not be a hunger for a faith unafraid of historical and scientific criticism? But by 1939, when the next great Conference met at Tambaram, the outlook had dramatically changed. On the one hand rising nationalisms had reawakened loyalties to the religions with which the newly self-conscious nations had long been associated; on the other hand, within the Christian Churches, urgent questions were being asked about the relation of those religions to God's crucial and critical word in and through Christ – did not that Word condemn as tragically misconceived all man-made religious attempts to gain acceptance with God apart from Christ?

The Second World War brought to an end a whole era of imperial expansionism within which the task of proclaiming the Christian gospel had been carried on under conditions of relative safety. Missionaries had been confident that the gospel was the source of enlightenment and progress and that ultimately pagan myths and rites would be seen to be incompatible with a true understanding of nature, man and God. But now, astonishingly, national and religious aspirations and affirmations were making common cause. The resurgence of non-Christian religions was one of the most significant phenomena of the post-war world.

Amongst those in the western world responsible for leadership within the missionary enterprise no one, I think, saw what was happening more clearly than did Max Warren, who had become General Secretary of the Church Missionary Society, the largest society within the Church of England. Through his speeches and writings, and particularly through his monthly News-Letters, he provided first-hand news of what was happening in world affairs and pleaded with his fellows and partners within the Church not to withdraw from the new situations but to seek in every way to stretch out towards those belonging to other faiths and to discover new aspects of God's purpose for the world by so doing. He was convinced that all was still under the control of God and that his people were being called upon to relate themselves creatively to these new developments. Ultimately he edited a series of books written mainly by those possessing expert knowledge of particular religions through having themselves been missionaries in the lands where they were practised. The writers shared his conviction that in approaching the devotee of another religion, the Christian was not seeking to imply that his neighbour knew nothing of God or that in no sense was the true God present. Rather both could assume that it was possible to enter into dialogue, each learning from the other the nature of his experience of God, trusting that in and through patient exchanges veils would be removed and the

Spirit of God would make luminous the face of Jesus Christ to whom the Christian missionary bore his witness.

I cite this particular example to illustrate what I believe has been *growth* in the attitude and approach to those belonging to other faiths. In the 1920s there was an outburst of enthusiasm in the Church of England for overseas missions. The World Call to the Church stressed the responsibility of all Christians to spread the gospel, to build up indigenous churches, to dispel idolatry and ignorance in the dark places of the earth. In many respects it was a splendid vision but it was too individualistic and too triumphalist. It did not allow for the responsibility which rests upon every true communicator to try to enter sympathetically and painstakingly into the language and symbol system of the other and thereby to relate his own message to the real conditions of the other's situation, culturally and religiously. By this method outward results may seem to be slower and less dramatic but if the faith of Christ is to enter deeply into the total life of a community and to act as a transforming agent, it is questionable whether there is any other way.

VI

I have written briefly about the Church's relation first to the world of science and technology and then to non-western cultures and religious traditions. What finally can be said about the Church's relation to and influence upon society inside England itself? Has it understood and come to terms with the rapid and far-reaching social changes that have been taking place? There can be no shadow of doubt that conditions in homes, in schools, in welfare agencies, in medical institutions, in industry, in the world of the arts, are vastly different today from what they were in 1924 when the notable Conference on Politics, Economics and Citizenship met in Birmingham under William Temple's chairmanship, or even in 1937 when the great international Conference on Church Community and State met in Oxford. The transformation of social structures since the Second World War has been phenomenal.

Probably at no point have members of the Church at large felt more deeply involved than in changes happening within family structures. Standards of sexual conduct, marriage and divorce, the status of women and their engagement in work outside the home, family planning and care of the aged — all these issues have concerned Christian leaders and especially those responsible for expounding the specifically Christian approach to them. One Lambeth Conference made a courageous declaration in regard to contraception; for a later Conference one of the most constructive reports of the post-war world on the family was produced. But there are long-established traditions within the Church, tenaciously held, celebrating on the one hand the virtues of motherhood, virginity, the procreation of children and wifely devotion, condemning on the other hand adultery, divorce, homosexuality and extra-marital intercourse. Has the Church manifested signs of *growth* in its attitude to these perplexing changes which have taken place in common outlooks within society at large?

There have certainly been immense resistances to change. At the same time there have been noteworthy signs that more liberal judgements in regard to broken marriages, family limitation and equality of status between men and women are now felt to be consonant with the mind of Christ. There has been no landslide towards permissiveness but rather an advance (which may at times have been over-cautious) towards the ideal of a comprehensive Christian community. So far the granting of equal status to women within the Church's priestly ministry has been refused by the House of Clergy within the General Synod. To one observer at least this can hardly be deemed a sign of *growth*. Many arguments, theological and pastoral, have been put forward in its favour since as long ago as the end of the First World War but the defenders of the *status quo* are still, it appears, in the majority.

In schools and colleges and in the Church's centres of education there has certainly been growth in enquiry about theories and practices in Religious Education. The bitter controversies which existed early in this century have been largely forgotten and first, by the famous Butler Act of 1944, a praiseworthy attempt was made to give every child some exposure to the Christian faith, and then, by widely representative Commissions in the 1960s, creative thought was given to how this could best be done. How could advances in methods of education in other disciplines be applied within the religious sphere? And because the personal equation is of such vital importance, how could teachers in schools and colleges be better equipped for their tasks?

Opinions will differ as to how far the Church of England has been wise, within the period we are considering, to retain Voluntary Aided Schools and Colleges of Education. Whether or not it has been wise, I do not think that any charge can be made that it has done so in a narrow, denominational spirit. Teachers have been trained to study the Bible and the history of Christianity by the help of the best available books by scholars of whatever allegiance. In the most difficult area of all — the Christian teacher's responsibility towards children nurtured in other faiths — there has been, so far as I am able to judge, a commendable willingness to gain information about those other faiths at first hand and to fulfil the teaching task in a comparative rather than a dogmatic spirit. There are bound to be dangers when any new policy is adopted but in general there has, I believe, been growth towards apprehension and comprehension in the colleges, however difficult it may have become either to gain sincere participation in school acts of worship or sustained interest in the classroom.

In relation to the bodily and mental health of the community and to the welfare and social services, I see few signs of growth in the Church's involvement. Indeed the obvious evidences are of supersession and withdrawal. The State has assumed ever-increasing responsibility in those areas and what were once regarded as legitimate concerns within the Church's pastoral ministry are now largely organized by and financed by the State. The danger here lies in the widespread conclusion that the Church's task is purely 'spiritual' or 'doctrinal' (i.e. confined to *verbal* declarations and confessions) with *sacramental* (i.e. the sanctification of material objects and bodily actions) ordinances retreating into the background. And what is assumed in the realm of bodily and mental health applies also in the sphere of *work*.

During this century, work has become increasingly mechanized and automated and has consequently appeared to have nothing to do with structures divinely created and directed. The gap which exists between the Church and organized labour is perhaps the most serious feature of our national life today. I have seen few signs in the past fifty years of growing understanding or empathy between on the one side the comprehension by the Church of God's purposes for society and on the other the theories of social structure and objectives espoused by management and labour, whether within the great nationalized industries or in those still geared to free enterprise.

Finally there is the fascinatingly interesting realm of the arts. How far has the Church progressed in its appreciation of artistic achievements and how far has it been able to find a place for creative art within its own organic life? The Churches, and perhaps in particular the Church of England, have inherited so noble a tradition from the past in architecture, in stained glass, in church furnishings, in literature and in music that their members find it far from easy to accept or relate themselves to new designs and compositions. The mordant New Testament phrase springs readily to contemporary lips: 'The old is better.'

Yet in spite of initial hesitations and continuing criticisms from the many, the pioneering few have discerned evidences in certain new works not only of artistic talent but also of deep insight into the mysteries of the Christian faith. George Bell, when Dean of Canterbury and later when Bishop of Chichester, did his utmost to enrich the life of the Church by drawing upon the talents of modern artists, notably those of T. S. Eliot, whose play *Murder in the Cathedral* proved to be one of the outstanding expressions of drama possessing religious depth. In turn Walter Hussey, who became Dean of Chichester, had the distinction of adding works by Henry Moore, Graham Sutherland and Benjamin Britten to the treasures of the Church and thereby of helping church members to grow in appreciation of visual and tonal patterns which may at first have seemed strange and even repellent.

I doubt whether the *standard* of church music, choral and instrumental, has ever been higher in England than it is at present, a situation which may be partly due to the challenges towards excellence presented by opportunities to broadcast and to provide music for special occasions. The fabric of historic churches has been preserved with perceptive care and every effort has been made to ensure that additions, when made, should be in harmony with the total artistry of the existing building. Attempts to construct new churches with modern materials and in modern style have provoked controversy but the Church has at least grown beyond the unquestioned assumption that Gothic style and cruciform shape were the only suitable patterns for a place of Christian worship.

Until comparatively recently in the history of mankind religion and the arts have been intimately associated with one another. Within the twentieth century, however, institutional religion has often failed to retain the allegiance of the most creative artists while dramatists, painters and novelists in particular have constantly chosen subjects which seem to have no place for or understanding of religious traditions and contemporary manifestations. In such a period, commerce between the worlds of religion and art has not been easy. Yet I believe that there have at least been pockets of growth in the Church of England in which the few have stretched out to embrace and draw into the ongoing stream of the Church's life works of beauty and insight, while men and women possessing notable artistic gifts have found within the life and worship of the Church a source of inspiration and a sustaining grace for their continuing labours.

The New Testament (apart from the Acts of the Apostles) has comparatively little to say about growth in numbers. But it speaks of growth in wisdom, in faith, in truth, in love, in grace and in the knowledge of our Lord and Saviour, Jesus Christ. It is in the Epistle to the Ephesians that the picture of growth is most clearly delineated, the Church being likened both to a growing temple and to a growing body. Such growth cannot be measured by figures and charts. Have we in the past fifty years grown in some measure in our apprehension of the Christ and our identification with him in worship, in wisdom and in witness? I cannot give any simple answer to that question. But I think there are signs that there has in fact been growth in ways of corporate worship, in a deepening understanding of Christian faith and in the sense of responsibility amongst church members at large to stretching out in love and compassion to the wider world with its manifold needs.

SIX

Signs of Growth in the Work of Mission

An appraisal through Anglican eyes

The Reverend Canon JAMES ROBERTSON,
General Secretary of U.S.P.G.

In the past decade, when the word 'growth' has been used in relation to the Church and mission, many Christians engaged in mission have based their work on an understanding of growth that was developed and expressed in the Bangkok Commission on World Mission and Evangelism Conference of 1973. There it was said that (Church) growth was 'at the same time (i) the numerical growth of the Church, (ii) the development of the new man, in every person; and (iii) the rooting of Christians' faith in local realities and their commitment to society'.

Anglicans gathered at Dublin in 1973 for the Second Anglican Consultative Council thought through these three aspects of growth and commented thus:

1. We are still commissioned to go to all the world. Each Church should be planning that the gospel should be spoken to this generation in language and categories that they can hear and understand. The resources of the older Churches should be shared with those Churches whose task is too great for them to manage alone.

2. Growth is to be measured in the maturing of each person so that he is able to do God's work. All programmes of teaching and training should aim at service and witness and not merely an intellectual or pietistic goal. It must be emphasized that service here is not thought of as merely service to the Church but service to God in the world. This service may be in evangelism; it may also be in such worlds as industry, politics, sport, and suburban life.

3. Those who are rooted in God must spread out into the realities of their society in two ways: to men and women as persons who need

renewal through reconciliation to God and re-making by his Spirit: and to structures of society which must be re-made to bring men into right relationships to each other as individuals and in groups. The work of the renewal of men and women through reconciliation should be done in fellowship with all who have been reconciled in Christ. The renewal of structures may be done in fellowship with any who share with Christians the desire to see a better order for any part of creation.

An analysis of these comments provides a remarkable catalogue of those aspects of Christian mission within which we may detect the signs of hope for our own renewal in mission as we work for the coming of the Kingdom of God. Let me try first to list these aspects and then portray from personal experience their world-wide visibility.

1. Numerical growth
2. The indigenization of the Church
3. Partnership in the sharing of resources
4. Equipping the people of God theologically
5. Service in the world
6. Reconciliation
7. Ecumenical co-operation
8. Fellowship with those outside the Church.

1. Numerical Growth

A headline in the Preparatory Information for the 1978 Lambeth Conference was '3,000 NEW ANGLICANS DAILY'. Closer scrutiny showed that this referred to the statistical count of 1,124,700 births within the Anglican community in 1977. From this needed to be deducted an estimated loss of 584,890 by death and of 308,090 by nett withdrawal from membership. So came the clearer figure of an average annual increase in membership between 1972 and 1977 of 231,720. This last figure of annual growth is set against an estimate in 1975 of

48,394,000 baptized
16,222,237 on communicants' roll
and 5,802,678 Easter communicants.

When we see these figures against total population figures for 1978 we get

World Population	4,170,107,000
Professing Anglicans	63,859,130
Anglican annual increase	231,720 (1977 figure).

So we grow as a family, but in no sense keep pace with population growth. In 1900 we were 2·1% of the world population. In 1978 we were 1·5% of the rapidly expanding general population.

To complete the picture it is important to remember the size of the other Christian communities:

Roman Catholic	765,000,000
Orthodox	155,000,000
Protestants	280,000,000
Independents (Third World)	66,000,000

The largest losses to Anglican Church membership are to be found in the older churches of the western world, and this applies to the major Catholic and Protestant Churches of the same regions. The growth places are Central Africa, Kenya, Papua New Guinea, Sudan, Tanzania, Uganda, Ruanda, Burundi and Zaire.

The last point to note is that annual baptisms have declined by 2·7% per annum since 1972, and correspondingly annual confirmations have been going down by 2·9% each year.

So in statistical terms there is slight growth absolutely, but not so proportionately, and this is a chastening fact. What signs of hope are there then under the aspect of numerical growth?

To me the significant change of mind to be detected is the recall, in the national churches of the Anglican Communion, to the duty laid upon us of evangelism. When the Anglican Consultative Council met in Canada in 1979 it reported concisely thus: (ACC–4, p. 17)

> The Lambeth Report, 1978, speaks (p. 55) of mission as 'embracing everything the Church is sent into the world to do'. Included in this 'everything' and lying at its heart is the proclaiming of Jesus as Saviour and Lord, by the Church, to the world. When the Church does this directly and deliberately it is engaged in evangelism. When it goes on

to minister in the world in acts of service and witness, it is animated by the same Gospel and proclaims the Word made Flesh in other ways. Evangelism, within mission, is thus explicit and implicit, intentional and permeating. The exchanges we have had with one another have made it clear that there is a call everywhere for this whole Gospel-based spirit to animate the mission-in-partnership which we want to emphasise.

Despite the internal impatience and misunderstandings that surround the present Nationwide Initiative in Evangelism in England, the animation within the sponsors reflects the recall to the great commission of our Lord in Matthew chapter 28.

Speaking with Bishops in Asia and Africa one recalls fragments spoken with conviction: 'I look for future priests with fire in their belly about their love for Jesus Christ.'

'I chided a young intellectual ordinand who was thin after a spell in the interior mission. He shook me when he replied, "Bishop, I may be thin in my body, but I am very fat in my heart."'

A recent visit to Singapore when the diocese was keeping its seventieth anniversary, showed a local church praising God for an upward swing in membership. An exhibition showed this chart:

Years	Average numbers of yearly Confirmations	Baptisms
1949–53	274	675
1959–68	383	1,303
1969–73	698	1,098
1974–75	1,408	1,985

A small indicator of numerical growth where the impetus to personal evangelism is constantly fostered.

It is also a fact that the rate of confirmations in an extremely poor country like Malawi, and a war-torn country like Zimbabwe in the ten years before legal independence far outstrips anything we are accustomed to in the West.

2. The Indigenization of the Church

One of the constant modern criticisms of mission has been the way in which western missionaries have contributed to the crushing of indigenous culture by presenting the gospel, and the visible Church, in terms of their own cultural forms, instead of baptizing the cultural patterns that were already there before Christian mission began. My own observation is that while the criticism is generally true, it is not just in all places and at all times. A lot depended on the theological stance of the corporate missionary group at particular moments in history. It is simplistic to imagine that the gospel can be shared without cultural exchange and even clash. There have been other powerful administrative, commercial, economic, recreational and artistic forces at work, challenging cultures. Too much is often laid at the door of 'mission' when the real culprits have been governments and the more obvious agents of a materialist, consumer-orientated, expansionist, technological culture in the West. However, organized mission shares the guilt to some degree.

It is this recognition of guilt, and fresh theological awareness, that has committed Christian mission agencies to promoting the indigenization of the Church.

There are at least three pointers to the implementing of this principle:

(a) Episcopal leadership in most places is now firmly in the hands of local, indigenous people. For example: in East Asia, including Burma, Japan and the Philippines, containing 55 episcopal dioceses there is only one expatriate western bishop; in Nigeria, Kenya and Tanzania, with 35 dioceses, all are indigenous men. Twenty years ago the figures would have been staggeringly different.

(b) Admittedly there are still pockets of Anglicanism where the outward forms of worship seem more centred on the Prayer Book of 1662 than the English at home are now accustomed to. However the trend in Asia and Africa is very much to offer indigenous singing and instrumental playing and dancing as an expression of Christian worship. The Queen's 1979 visit to Holy Cross Cathedral, Lusaka, Zambia, meant a sharing of African liturgical music of an order quite different from that her Mother experienced when she laid the foundation stone of the same Cathedral in 1957.

The emergence of the South East Asia Institute for Liturgy and Music in Manila – directed by Francisco F. Feliciano for the encouragement of Asian music and arts in the service of liturgy – is another example of the vision of all cultures making their offering in Christian worship.

(c) It is significant that it was a group of Christian leaders in Africa who invited the Reverend Adrian Hastings to produce his influential volume *Christian Marriage in Africa* (SPCK 1973). This whole enterprise shows how strongly the young Church in Africa has felt the need to be fulfilling and not destroying at a major point in African civilization where there has been constant clash with historic western Christian norms.

3. Partnership in the Sharing of Resources

Since the meeting in 1973 of the Anglican Consultative Council in Dublin, the Anglican Church has committed itself publicly and purposively to a resource-sharing philosophy that has come to be called 'Partnership in Mission'. The phrase is intended to promote the death of the idea that we are split into donor churches and receiver churches. We are one Church, with one mission, and a complementary partnership with one another, at all levels, is to be the style of our engagement with the world.

There has thus been inaugurated a process of joint consultation 'based on the conviction that both giving and receiving must extend throughout the whole family of Anglican churches, and that every church will receive others as its partners in mission with the variety of resources which they have to offer' (ACC–2, p. 55).

The practical implementation of these ideas began in 1974 with the inauguration of a series of Partners-in-Mission Consultations in Anglican provinces all over the world. By 1980 there had taken place twenty-six such events, and some of these are already in a second phase. The Church of England, complex in history and present structure, is preparing for its first national Partners-in-Mission Consultation in 1981. It is already beginning to experience something of the loosening and reshaping of relationship bonds that comes to any church which participates in the process.

Partners are seen to be neighbouring dioceses and not just overseas agencies. Fresh frankness appears about resources and the attitude that frees resources and re-deploys them more efficiently.

Old insights are rediscovered and freshly appropriated. 'We need to widen our understanding of the resources which we have to share. They extend beyond money and personnel. Our partnership is grounded first of all in our fellowship in the gospel, and all the gifts we have to share are an expression of that fellowship and a means of deepening it. Ideas become resources; experience from experimental projects can be shared; other cultures have gifts to bring, and the spiritual maturity and experience of Christians in one place can be the inspiration and encouragement of those elsewhere.' (ACC-4, p. 26)

Personal examples of this come to mind. I remember the simple testimony of Christians from Burma, at a 1979 Partners-in-Mission Consultation in Hong Kong, about their growth in spirituality since they had to learn self-reliance without external missionary personnel, after the virtual closure of their country to western agencies. I rejoiced when I heard the diocese of Singapore renounce a particular request for financial help to a project, because it saw how the need of a neighbouring diocese was greater. The older bilateral tradition of discussion would never have unearthed these signs of growth in a maturity to be promoted and rejoiced in.

The inauguration in England of the Partnership for World Mission in late 1978 is another sign of the way in which the partnership principle has been educative at home. The traditional missionary societies of the Church of England have formed a co-operative partnership with Synod to help co-ordinate the response by the Church here to its sister churches throughout the world. Many younger churches only knew the Church of England through a particular society, but they aspire to talk with, and co-operate with the whole Church. Synod itself is a relatively new organ of the whole Church of England. With the Societies there is formed a forum for co-ordination and joint planning that must surely have an effect on the Societies themselves and their complementary and sometimes competitive relationships. Not only that, it brings into the fellowship of world mission societies that have traditionally had a 'home' image, like the Church Army and the Mothers' Union.

One fair criticism of this process towards mission-in-partnership is that the emphasis on Anglican co-operation in world mission, in every continent, has not yet been matched by ecumenical involvement. Because Partners-in-Mission has started as a 'family' enterprise it has perhaps inevitably been over-successful in developing Anglican fellowship, and sense of identity, at the expense of local ecumenical co-operation in mission.

The 1973 ACC-2 ideals were clearly expressed: 'The projects and activities already being carried out or planned by other denominations in the area should also be considered in the planning process. Wherever and whenever possible joint action for mission and ecumenical sharing of personnel should be undertaken. Any truly comprehensive plan will only be possible if related to the life and work of other denominations, governments and voluntary agencies.' (ACC-2; p. 57) The only encouraging thing is that in churches where the second phase of the consultation process has begun, there is a growing readiness to press the ecumenical questions. As we shall see in the next section, it is perhaps at the level of preparation for ministry that most signs of growth are to be discerned.

Lest this account end on too gloomy a note it is worth recounting one little known enterprise in ecumenical mission. In Botswana, an Anglican priest, Ronald Wynne, has for the past ten years been living with a group of Africans who came over from Angola during the war there, to settle across a border that was not of their creating. They are the Hambukushu people, thirteen villages, numbering 4,500 persons. He works under the aegis of the Botswana Christian Council. He has brought their language into a systematic written and grammatical form (*English/Mbukushu Dictionary*, published by Avebury Publishing Company 1980). During his life with them he has brought about half of them into the Christian fellowship. He has steadfastly refused to bring them into a denomination. When the time came for their baptism into the Christian Church he made certain that Rome and Geneva approved the liturgy of baptism. Theirs has been a re-enactment in a few years of the Hebrew evolution of an understanding of the People of God and of our understanding of how in Jesus Christ God 'has visited and redeemed his people'. He went back in 1979 to continue his ministry to lead them into the sacramental life, and confessed that he could not yet foresee how this would work out in practice.

Perhaps he and his people are a microcosm of the very themes we have already been examining; numerical growth, indigenization, and partnership.

4. Equipping the People of God, Theologically

A sectional group at the meeting of the Fourth Anglican Consultative Council in London, Ontario, Canada, during May 1979, had as its topic 'A Theological Basis of Human Rights'. When they first reported in plenary session a fascinating encounter took place between the group and all the other members. They had chosen a case history approach to their theological study. It did not go down well when presented. The majority could not comprehend that the method was truly theological. The group was sent back to reflect again. They chose to record their dilemma thus:

> Our next question was how best to provide them and ourselves with the Christian insights and values, based on God's revelation to man through Jesus Christ, so as to inspire them with vision, motivate them with love, and sustain them with courage and hope in their struggles and sufferings. It was a question of how we should engage in providing a theological basis. Should we begin with an explicit and systematic statement of the Christian doctrines of God, man, and the world, and of the person and work of Jesus Christ, drawing out the necessary implications of human rights in general and in particular situations? Or should we first consider a variety of situations relating to the struggle for human rights which we had either experienced. . .? Should we then consider how the record of God's dealing with mankind in the world and especially through Jesus Christ could provide us with fundamental insights and values that would focus our vision and motivate our response. . .?

They went on to choose the method '*that would focus attention on God, but as experienced from within the human situation*'.

I recount this process at length because it characterizes the theological style of the world Church in the present age, when it comes to equipping its people for their encounter with the world. Its strands are experiential, situational, biblical, historical and letting theological truth grow out of the encounter.

The emergence of liberation theology in Latin America, of black theology in the United States and South Africa, of Asian and Africans theologies, are all signals that the style has become inductive rather than deductive. The literature is already extensive, and it would be out of place to do more than note the direction of theological momentum.

Probably the most influential example of this trend in mission circles is to be seen in the 'theological education by extension' movement. It had been felt that those trained in an enclosed seminary or theological school system were ill-prepared to grapple with the existential turmoil in the lives of those to whom they ministered. They had developed a corpus of knowledge, a technical language, and a set of conceptual categories which prevented their rapport with those whom they were to serve, living in the real world of power conflicts and ethical chaos.

In Central America they were encouraged to inter-leave short spells of study with practical, reflective work among people, testing out their biblical grasp against the felt realities of the people to whom they were to be pastors. Field tutorial help supplemented their own personal explorations. The system provided for periodic returns to base. The textual and the contextual became interwoven in their lives.

I have seen this working in quite small diverse places. The Tokyo Anglican seminary has on its staff a lay field placement officer concerned with finding relevant experience situations for students and developing their capacity to learn theologically within them. The young lay parish assistants, men and women, trained in the Seminari Theologika Malaysia, have always had similar field experiences integral with their study sessions. One of the most vigorous movements is that called Theological Education by Extension. Pioneered in Latin America, it insisted that the learning process for theological students be related to their local situations, as a lifelong exercise, and not simply a short spell of academic study. 'Education is decentralized, carried out in small groups, mostly for ordinary folks who want to add greater depths of understanding to their Christian faith.' Special materials are prepared. Study centres are scattered in many areas. The South American Missionary Society has helped produce material, Study by Extension for All Nations. Feed the Minds, the Society for Promoting Christian Knowledge and the United Society for Christian Literature have all been generous with literature support. South Africa, Malawi and parts of India have latterly followed the Theological Education by Extension example.

These examples are, of course, even less significant world-wide than the work done by the Theological Education Fund (1958–77) of the World Council of Churches. This set of programmes developed the whole theme of 'contextuality' in a powerful manner. The Fund's work in encouraging the development of ecumenical, large-scale, and academically rigorous institutions, rooted authentically in local situations is a remarkable achievement in twenty years. In the last three years the emphasis has developed in the Programme for Theological Education, of bringing the more established, traditional theological institutions in the western world into a dialogue with the Third World institutions, and their response to local situations. We might well see nearer home a re-orientation of theological centres as resource places for laity and clergy, on a continuing learning basis.

Indeed some indications are already here: the Urban Theology Unit at Sheffield, the Urban Ministry Project at Morden, the Stepney Action Research Team, and the Urban Church Project are all examples.

Perhaps the enterprise that needs to be better and more widely known is the Department of Mission of the Selly Oak Colleges, in Birmingham. There the staff of four traditional missionary colleges have combined ecumenically (within the wider Federation of Selly Oak), and in conjunction with central staff, to provide programmes in a community setting, for mission education. The students comprise many from the Third World doing in-service training, British students preparing for church service in other cultures, mainland European students making a bridge into British culture as a step towards overseas service elsewhere, and mid-service missionaries reflecting on their field experiences. Their studies range over many disciplines, biblical, systematic theology, anthropology, social studies, etc. They generate a community of interaction between cultures, between young and old, between married families and single people that is quite unique in British education, and they have an opportunity to share in a multi-cultural Christian worship that both makes the offering to God and binds the participants together. They have developed special living issues courses, and mission modules that are open to short-term students from within the British churches.

5. Service in the World

This aspect of our short survey is necessarily linked with the previous section. If our equipping of the people of God were only for service in the Church we should be engaged in a sterile, truncated enterprise.

Thankfully Christian mission has for long been characterized by some quite remarkable service in compassionate works of mercy. The whole witness of medical missions, general, and specialized (for example, towards Leprosy and Blindness), is well known and needs no underlining. Similarly its witness in education, particularly at pioneering levels, is globally known.

There is, however, a great diversity of other ways in which service in the world has been developed. If one looks at the skills asked for by younger churches it is illuminating to see how missionary service can take interesting modern guises. Speaking a short time ago with a television producer interested in making a documentary on missionaries, I remember his astonishment when my colleagues spoke about a potter whom we had been asked to provide, now working in Malawi.

But much more significant than the diverse skills and professions asked for is the important enterprise, ecumenically based, which is

called Christians Abroad. This small organization starts out with
the vision that in modern days much of the best missionary work is
done when people, following their own trades, professions and
vocations, go abroad on mainly secular terms of exchange and
employment, and witness to their faith by identifying with the
local church in whatever country they are placed. They have no
'professional' ecclesiastical ministry, but they represent the univer-
sality of the Christian fellowship in a quite remarkable – and
natural – way. Christians Abroad keeps this vision in front of the
committed, helps some to find employment in secular tasks,
informs men, women and their families about conditions overseas,
and commends them to known contacts there. Already the
exploration is made beyond traditional work like teaching to
offering a service of preparation and information to secular firms.
At this level they begin to touch a parallel enterprise at Farnham
Castle, called The Centre for International Briefing, where
residential courses are provided for anyone contemplating a period
of service overseas, whether animated specifically within the
Christian fellowship or not.

Even this work, encouraging sign that it is, has only a small
significance compared with the development of service in the
world by local Christians everywhere in their own place. I can
think of a small unit in Karachi, and another in Delhi, where an
advisory service to working men and women about their legal
rights in employment, has given hope for the future to many; of
the social outreach to pavement dwellers and displaced people
pioneered from Calcutta Cathedral by the late Subir Biswas; of the
ministry of Hong Kong Christian Service to a transit camp of Boat
People from Vietnam, numbering between nine and ten thousand
people; of at least two parishes in Malaysia where a night class opportunity for study given to young adolescents transforms their
chance of making the grade in school work; of a school for the
mentally and physically handicapped in Seoul, Korea, founded
and developed by a Korean priest and his English wife. The
catalogue is endless. There are hundreds of thousands of Christian
service frontiers all over the world.

6. Reconciliation

The classic text for this aspect of growth is 2 Corinthians 5. 18–20 (RV): 'But all things are of God, who reconciled us to himself through Christ, and gave unto us the ministry of reconciliation; to wit that God was in Christ reconciling the world unto himself, not reckoning unto them their trespasses, and having committed unto us the word of reconciliation.' In mission this reconciliation is often thought of as that activity of grace in which man is reconciled to God, to his fellow men, and to the whole of creation.

We have already commented on that aspect of mission we call evangelism, as it is related to the numerical growth of the Church. But modern mission is suspicious of any understanding of evangelism which is individualist and concentrates solely on a salvation thought of as private and individual. ACC-4 (p. 18) put the wider view in these words:

> The evangelism to which Christians are committed belongs first to the Church as a whole in its apostolic character. The Church expresses it both corporately, and in persons, and tries to do so in a variety of ways. Sometimes evangelism will have its focus in a person-to-person exchange using the words of the Lord and of the people of God through history. But it will also go well beyond this in the challenging judgements which Christians make, in the name of Christ and with the authority of the Gospel, to the whole life of society in our contemporary world. To recapture the width of the evangelistic action of the Church is a necessary part of our good news for the age.

Where then can we see the Church in action as a reconciling force? The examples are legion and any choice has to be arbitrary and subjective.

Possibly the most vivid example is of the Church in Uganda in the post-Amin period. We saw Anglicans and Roman Catholics planning together and identifying solidly with the damaged nation in its commitment to reconstruction. Yet even as one writes (May 1980) the magnitude of the task, and cyclical reversal into greedy conflict, is a reminder that reconciliation is a process more than an act.

We are beginning to hear of the efforts of the Churches in Canada taking their stand with the Indian and Esquimaux people in relation to land rights and reparation programmes. Comparable action is reported from New Zealand in regard to the Maori people, and in Australia for the aborigine groups. So often these identifications are seen publicly as strife-centred, when in truth the motive and end are concerned with reconciling people in the grip of unjust historical heritages.

The world problems of racism, class conflict, affluence and destitution, rape of natural resources, competitive armed powers, etc. all have Christian cells pressing their gospel case as part of the mission of the Church. A dead Steve Biko and a living Desmond Tutu in South Africa are recognized as reconcilers. Quaker groups in New York and Geneva work quietly but systematically to promote the talking between adversaries that is better than warring. The hidden work of the World Council of Churches in the Sudan a year or two ago is recognized as instrumental in the reconciliation achieved there. Many Africans see the grants of the Programme to Combat Racism as the only sign for them that the Christian Church takes the ministry of reconciliation seriously. What has impressed the western world about Mr Robert Mugabe in Zimbabwe has been his capacity to articulate words of reconciliation in marked contrast to reported extremisms in an earlier phase. Where does this come from if not from a grasp of what is good news for people in an education given earlier within the Roman Catholic Church?

It would be idle to assume that Christian mission is not always conscious of its failures in reconciliation. For the British people Northern Ireland is a constant reminder of the divisiveness of a Christianity which chooses arrogant dogma of any extreme kind. But at the same time the ground swell of change there has a Christian vision behind it and the will to reconcile refuses to die.

A most imaginative analysis of the British scene today is contained in the British Council of Churches' sustained study 'Britain Today and Tomorrow'. It is the fruit of personal and group study by Christians over a period of several years and is summarized admirably in a paper-back with the same title by T. Beeson (Fount

Paperback, Collins 1978). It was meant to be the analytical prelude
to a more sustained programme of practical reconciliation work by
British Christians. But we do not rise to the challenges, except in
tiny cells of effort.

The signs of hope are there, but the animation of the reconciling
body awaits renewal by the Spirit of God.

7. Ecumenical Co-operation

Once or twice above we have referred to positive and negative
signs in relation to this aspect of mission. We rejoice in the
examples of witness shown by Ronald Wynne and by 'Christians
Abroad'. We are sad about the apathy shown towards the report
'Britain Today and Tomorrow'.

But in a wonderful way we keep the ecumenical vision alive.
The recent pastoral Congress of the Roman Catholic Church in
England (Liverpool 1980) passed a recommendation that the
Roman Church should become members of the British Council of
Churches. That identification in fullness would do much to
transform the scene.

We await the publication of the report on covenanting towards
unity by the churches involved therein. We see the rapid growth
of local ecumenical projects (325 now in England). There is serious
talk about an ecumenical Bishop for Swindon where ecumenism
has found a sturdy way forward.

The Pope and the Archbishop of Canterbury can meet in Ghana
and take counsel as friends. The Archbishop can be enthroned in
Canterbury surrounded by witnesses in fellowship from the
corners and denominations of the world.

When reconstruction in Zimbabwe is needed, the appeal that
goes to British Christians is made in totally ecumenical terms,
something that has not before been so publicly evident and authentic.

The movement towards church union in the organic sense has
fluctuations in its momentum. North India, South India and
Pakistan represent the stoutest efforts towards national church

unity, with plenty of heartbreaks in the continued effort of learning to live in amity.

The ecumenical agencies for compassionate care are highly respected for their co-operative work. The Commission on Inter-Church Aid, the Refugee and World Service of the World Council of Churches has a programme budget of approximately £20 million in the present year. Christian Aid and the Catholic Fund for Overseas Development have grown in significance and magnitude with the years. The present reconstruction programmes in Zimbabwe are marvellously served by Christian Care, the service organization of the Zimbabwe Council of Churches.

This aspect of growth makes possible Christian action on a macro-scale which adds significantly to the atomistic efforts of a multitude of smaller mission agencies more traditionally involved. It has admirably enriched the expressions of Christian service to which the gospel impels us.

8. Fellowship with Those Outside the Church

The jargon phrase which comes to mind is 'Dialogue with peoples of other faiths and ideologies'. Of course this process has always been going on quietly on a person-to-person basis, sometimes scholarly and sometimes devotional. But in latter years there has emerged a fresh sense of purpose in reaching towards one another in a world often described as a global village. The causes of this are legion: the end of colonial empires, the nomadic movements of populations because of trade, wars, easier travel, immigration needs for labour, telecommunications, etc.

Britain itself is recognized, and grows to recognize itself, as a plural society, multi-faith, multi-national, multi-cultural and multi-racial. There are plenty of evidences of the conflicts engendered when practical issues like education, future immigration, inter-marriage, unemployment, and social mores begin to emerge.

There has been early perception in Britain of the need for ecumenical initiative in this area. The Committee for Relations with People of Other Faiths within the British Council of Churches is the major organ for initiating the dialogue that is necessary, and suggesting which themes inside our common life require most research and guidance. At a more practical level the Community and Race Relations Unit of the Division of Community Affairs of the British Council of Churches concerns itself with analysis and practical help in the socio-political field. These groups keep in close touch with the Boards and Councils of the main stream churches at appropriate levels. What all have in common is the perception that when facing the questions posed by a plural society, the Church is challenged to apply itself to a significant aspect of mission today, in the name of Jesus Christ.

Manifestly the stance of the Christian community is significantly different in those parts of the world where a 'missionary' faith or ideology is closely identified with the state and nation, and with the declared attitude of the state towards the Christian religion and towards conversion.

When the Anglican Consultative Council met in Canada in 1979 and the topic of 'Islam' was raised it was remarkable how diverse were the attitudes expressed. Those who worked in Pakistan, Malaysia and the Middle East found it hard to express a common rationale, as the following quotation (Report, p. 24) indicates:

> We have taken note of the fact of the religious revival of Islam in the world. In some parts of the world Christians have met with varying degrees of pressure and tolerance. It is therefore important to discover in depth the common theological factors with Islam, recognising that such basic common factors are basic for responsible dialogue and interaction. The style of the dialogue and its concerns are bound to be both cultural and theological. Means must therefore be found to take such dialogue forward ecumenically, using cross-cultural and international experience as much as possible, especially when facing common materialistic and secular challenges.

To some this kind of comment may seem over-bland, but at least it breathes an eirenic spirit in happy contrast to that of earlier ages in history.

Here in Britain, the work of the Centre for the Study of Islam and Christian-Muslim Relations, under the direction of David Kerr, at the Selly Oak Colleges, Birmingham, is a splendid pointer to the seriousness with which this aspect of the general theme is receiving rigorous and sympathetic attention. (The report of the Conference on 'Christian Mission and Islamic Da'wah', 1976, in vol. lxv No. 260, of the *International Review of Mission*, gives an excellent introduction to the sensitivities involved.)

When it comes to other faiths and ideologies the witness of the Church in India in the face of possible proscription through legislation proposed (1978–9) about religious conversions is to be noted. The Christians were quick to see how administrative interpretation of what seemed to be a simple and secularly fair law could have led to a severe restriction of human rights. In countries like Mozambique, where a Marxist political ideology prevails, the Church has been impelled to think through how Christians bear their witness in a state which moved almost overnight from a harsh Christian theocracy to an avowedly communist regime. Marvellously it evoked in 1979 this most hopeful letter from the Anglican Bishop, Dinis Sengulane:

My beloved brethren,

I wonder whether we are aware of the deep implications, in matters of faith, of belonging to the Christian era and of being a Christian?

What we mean by saying that we are in 1979 of the Christian Era is that in all those years since Christ's birth, a new essence of life, a life which cannot be crushed down by pressures (physical or spiritual), not an easy life, has begun. It is a life of a sure and accomplished victory through Him who loved us. As I look at the history where so much folly has gone by, through and in Christianity, and yet Christ has always shone, as I know He is faithful, I can shout with joyful tears: Yes Lord, I want to be part of that Christian Era and I praise You that You are the same today and always.

You will be shocked with some of the news now reaching you. You may ask: 'Why such contradictions of signs of powerlessness and powerfulness? Why such signs of powers of darkness that seem to be the order of the day, even when we know and feel the reality of the victory of the powers of light?'.

We are in 1979 of the Era of Christ, not after Christ as if Christ is overdue, outdated. We are in Christ, and 'the disciple is not above his teacher, nor a servant above his master; it is enough for the disciple to be like his teacher and the servant like his master'. Christ's Era means that we are to be ready to face what Christ had to face; to be Christ-like in our lives.

When this letter was read in the presence of Her Majesty The Queen, in St Botolph's Church on 6 March 1980, when the United Society for the Propagation of the Gospel and the Society for Promoting Christian Knowledge were giving thanks on the 250th anniversary of their founder, the congregation heard it 'like a New Testament Epistle'.

Readers will quickly perceive that what has been sketched in relation to the plural society, Islam and ideology, is all the more applicable to China, but to do more than note this is impossible in one chapter of a book. ACC4 (Report, p. 23) commented:

> It is still difficult to assess the significance of what appears to be a change of climate in that country towards certain other nations and the practice of religion. If a new openness to outside contacts becomes a fact, perhaps the greatest difficulty on the part of the Church will be to restrain misguided enthusiasm. The whole Church may be strengthened through receiving from the Church in China something of their experience during the many years of isolation and persecution.

Conclusion

It happens that this chapter is being completed in the month in 1980 when the successor to the commission on World Mission and Evangelism Conference held in Bangkok in 1973, is ending at Melbourne. Its great prayerful theme has been 'Your Kingdom Come'. We await its reports. It would seem from the sectional themes that it will not have focused on growth in numerical terms; it will certainly take forward 'the development of the new man in every person' and 'the rooting of Christians' faith in local realities and their commitment to society'.

The themes are themselves illuminating:

1. Good News to the Poor
2. The Kingdom of God and Human Struggle
3. The Church Witnesses to the Kingdom
4. The Crucified Christ Challenges Human Power.

They would seem to point to key issues for the age: Poverty and Affluence; Human Conflicts; Power, the Powers, and Powerlessness. These are the 'local realities' of a global village world. Unless these are faced the birth 'of the new man in every person' is made hard for millions, and 'numerical growth of the Church' is blocked, or worse still is kept unreal.

But even these 'ideas' are not the only background to this chapter. Famine in Asia and north-east Africa has reached mammoth proportions; racial strife in South Africa is reaching the edge of bloodbath; Afghanistan and Iran symbolize the kind of ideological and power hatreds which can be seen on every continent.

Against these our 'signs of growth' seem to many perhaps trivial, domestic, even superficial; they are realities 'no bigger than a man's hand'. But they signify a leaven at work within the community of faith which is itself in union with him who makes all things new. They are written down to keep us also a hope community, ready to be offered more fully as a love community, 'till we all come in the unity of the faith, and of the knowledge of the Son of God, unto the measure of the stature of the fulness of Christ'.

SEVEN

Grow or Die

The Reverend Canon ALEXANDER WEDDERSPOON
Canon of Winchester

In his poem 'Church going' Philip Larkin tells how, after visiting an English country church,

> I sign the book, donate an Irish sixpence,
> Reflect the place was not worth stopping for,
> Yet stop I did; in fact I often do,
> And always end much at a loss like this,
> Wondering what to look for; wondering, too,
> When churches fall completely out of use
> What shall we turn them into, if we shall keep
> A few cathedrals chronically on show,
> Their parchment, plate and pyx in locked cases,
> And let the rest rent-free to rain and sheep,
> Shall we avoid them as unlucky places?[1]

The previous essays in this book make clear that the poet's question is untimely. Bishop John Taylor, Bishop Colin James and Dr John Gray have all shown that churches in Britain are nowhere near falling completely out of use; the Dean of St Paul's has shown that cathedrals are busier than ever before in the whole of their history.

But the fact must still be faced that despite many examples of liveliness, the institutional church in Britain has been in steady decline for decades and in steep decline since the late 1960s. Some of the relevant facts and figures have been provided in the Introduction (p. 1). The extent of the decline varies somewhat between denominations, and limitations of space demand that this essay be restricted to the special problems of the Church of

England. As the Established Church it has a tradition of pastoral concern for all who call themselves 'C. of E.', whether they are active church members or not. This presents particular difficulties – and opportunities – and in this respect the (Anglican) Church of England corresponds more closely to the (Presbyterian) Church of Scotland than to any of the other denominations in England.

Awareness of the Church's decline has evoked a wide variety of responses in recent years. The Evangelical wing of the Church – a growing, vigorous and confident group – strongly urges traditional methods of evangelism and is enthusiastically behind the 'Nationwide Initiative in Evangelism' proposed by a representative group of church leaders in 1979. An example of Evangelical initiative was a much publicized campaign by Billy Graham in the Universities of Oxford and Cambridge in 1980. At the other end of the ecclesiastical spectrum, 'Anglo-Catholics' are committed to 'Catholic Renewal', which one of its publications describes as 'a movement within the Church of England which proclaims the Catholic faith . . . the whole faith and not just those bits which the fashions of an age find acceptable; its opposite is narrow, partial and sectarian.'

Others of a more radical standpoint will have nothing to do with either evangelism or Catholic renewal. They claim that the decline of the Church is to be welcomed as inevitable and positively desirable. They argue that the Church was never meant to be more than a dedicated, serving minority, a 'saving remnant', and that anxiety about numbers and 'success' is irrelevant triumphalism.

Others would argue that what is required of the Church is a steadfast faithfulness to the Lord in worship, teaching and pastoral care; that the Church is God's Church to grow or decline as he wills and that crusades, campaigns and ways of renewal are of no lasting significance.

The decline of the Church is the outcome of a complex interaction of cultural and institutional factors. There is no one simple cause. Among the more significant cultural factors may be included:

the secularization of thought and attitude which has resulted from the spectacular achievements of science, medicine and technology together with the development of behavioural sciences such as psychology and sociology.

the revolution which has taken place during the past century in beliefs about the authority of the Bible.

the variety of scholarly approaches to the central beliefs of Christian doctrine, creating an impression of theological doubt and confusion.

the sexual revolution, with its influence on attitudes to marriage and its challenge to traditional Christian standards.

an increasing awareness of the other great religions of the world, seen as belief systems in their own right rather than as heresies.
the corrosive influence of war, together with a long period of political and economic decline.

The reasons for the Church's decline have been analysed many times; the tragedy is that reasons have come to be regarded as *excuses*. Anglicans have succeeded in building around themselves a prison wall of negative thinking fifty feet high and topped with barbed wire.

Church administrators facing the organizational and financial problems of decline produced in 1974 what has become known as 'The Sheffield Report'. This presented a scheme for the fairer distribution of available manpower involving the closure of many churches, the amalgamation of others and a drastic measure of clergy rationing. The underlying assumption of the report was that decline is inevitable and that the Church must plan accordingly. The policies advocated differed little from those that any business management might adopt when faced with decline in demand, cash flow problems, loss of staff morale and an excess of retail outlets.

Decline has been gradual, a process of steady attrition rather than dramatic closures or spectacular bankruptcies. For the most part, bishops, clergy and lay people have plodded faithfully on with what has come to be accepted as the normal routine of 'church life'. No bishop or priest has, yet, been declared redundant; the decline in the numbers of clergy is the result of 'natural wastage' caused by retirement and death.

It is important to realize that members of the Church of England in general, and those in positions of leadership in particular, are sheltered from the harsher realities of decline by the very substantial and well-managed endowments of the Church Commissioners. Barely credible as it may seem to observers from other churches, both the Archbishops, all the Bishops, all the Deans, all the Provosts, all the Archdeacons, and about one half of the rest of the clergy could continue to live in their official houses and draw their salaries *even if no one went to church at all*. The Church of England's most consistently generous supporters are the faithful departed.

Under these circumstances, it is hardly surprising to find that the need to face the challenge of decline has not been the Church's top priority in recent years. But this is not to say that the Church's ordained and lay leaders have been idle – far from it. During the 1970s they have been busy with problems of internal reorganization, liturgical reform, ecumenical relations and with a wide range of difficult social, educational and moral issues, such as race relations, marriage and divorce, religious education, abortion and euthanasia. On the few occasions when the renewal of the Church has been publicly debated – as in the General Synod in November 1977 – there has been a realistic awareness of the complexity of the problem, a humbling sensitivity to past failures and an absence of any generally agreed response.

What then is to be done if the Church of England is not to decline permanently into a small, cultured, middle-class sect, a harmless ecclesiastical curiosity kept alive by the endowments of medieval benefactors?

What follows is essentially a personal statement. No other contributor to this book is committed in any way whatsoever to the suggestions which follow.

I believe that the principles of the church growth movement will, over the years, provide an effective way of renewal for the Church of England, *always assuming that these principles are in-*

telligently adapted to the realities of the British situation. The importance of that qualification cannot be overestimated.

The principles and methods of church growth are essentially *non-party*; they are applicable to Evangelicals, Anglo-Catholics and to those who believe that the sufficient term 'Anglican' includes that which is best in both the Catholic and Reformed traditions. They represent a way of renewal which would serve to unite rather than to divide. In the face of the severe decline which has afflicted the Church in recent years, they provide the one response which the Church has most significantly lacked — a coherent, positive and effective policy.

Origins of the Church Growth Movement

During the 1930s an American missionary, Donald McGavran, and a group of colleagues were at work in the plains of central India. After some years of evangelistic effort they began to find themselves increasingly puzzled by the varying degrees of effectiveness shown by different churches and denominations. They began to ask themselves such questions as:

(a) Why do some churches grow when others in the same area do not?
(b) Why does the same church grow at one time and not at another?
(c) Why do some denominations within the church grow while others do not?

In seeking answers to these questions they tried to gather information from all sources, religious and secular, and they refused to be satisfied with pious evasions like 'It was not the Lord's will', or 'The field was not ripe unto harvest.'

After many years of further missionary work and research, McGavran returned to the U.S.A. where he founded the Institute for Church Growth as a centre for study and research relating to the work of overseas missions. In 1965 the Institute became an established part of the School of World Mission at Fuller Theological Seminary in Pasadena, California. Fuller Seminary is a non-denominational college of Evangelical foundation, with a fine record of scholarship and a positive concern for missionary endeavour. As the work of the Institute developed, it quickly became apparent that the sort of questions being asked about church growth in the work of overseas missions were no less relevant to the problems facing the main line churches in America. This realization occurred at a time in the late 1960s when, for the first time in the twentieth century, many of the large American denominations began to decline both in numbers and confidence. The outcome of this was the development of a school of church growth specifically concerned with the problems of the churches in North America; many of the largest denominations in the U.S.A., including Methodists, Baptists and Episcopalians, established church growth departments to formulate growth principles in terms most applicable to their own denominations and theological emphases. At the same time, the study of church growth in the U.S.A. became an established subject at Fuller Seminary and a constituent part of the course leading to the award of the college's post-graduate degree of Doctor of Ministry.

A further development was the establishment of the Institute for American Church Growth, an independent non-denominational organization under the direction of Dr Winfield Arn, a man whose commitment to church growth arose – significantly – from his experience in the field of Christian education. The Institute concentrates on the running of training courses for church leaders and lay persons of all denominations; the staff of the Institute also travel the country initiating church growth programmes at local and parish level.

The church growth movement is of relatively recent origin and has, so far, made little impact in Britain. It has evoked some interest in Evangelical and Pentecostal churches, and much important pioneering work has been done by individuals like the Reverend E. Gibbs of the Bible Society. His course on 'What makes churches grow' has been used with profit by various churches of different denominations.

It has to be recognized that there are many in the Church of England who view the church growth movement with suspicion on the grounds that it has largely developed in North America. This suspicion is very understandable. Church leaders who have struggled for years with the problems of the church in decayed inner city areas, in depressed northern industrial towns and in bleak Fenland villages can be forgiven for looking askance at a movement which they associate with the big, busy churches of affluent middle-class America. It is certain that church growth will make no real progress in Britain until a specifically British school of church growth develops, using language and concepts acceptable to members of British churches, undergirded by intelligent theology and drawing on British research and experience.

Moreover, when a church has been in decline for decades it is disconcerting to be faced with the challenge of growth. Churches do not grow in England because no one any longer expects them to grow; decline has become a way of life and clergy and laity have adapted to it. But Canon James Robertson's essay has made clear that *decline is not a feature of the world-wide Church* — it is a characteristic of churches influenced by the secularization of thought and culture which has taken place in Western Europe. The fact remains: if the Church of England is not to decline permanently into an insignificant sect kept alive by the endowments of medieval benefactors, then the challenge of growth has to be faced.

Definition

'Church growth' may very briefly be defined as: 'All that is involved in bringing men and women into relationship with God, fellowship with Jesus Christ, the life of the Spirit, and active church membership'.

The study of church growth draws its content from a wide range of different disciplines: biblical studies, theology, mission studies, educational and pastoral studies, the social sciences and the study of management. While fully acknowledging the value of the pioneering work done by Dr Donald McGavran, and carried forward by his disciples, it must be recognized that the study of church growth has long since outgrown its missionary, academic and Evangelical origins. It is now, quite rightly, the concern of all who care for the renewal of the world wide church.

The Theology of Church Growth

The Christian Church began nineteen centuries ago with eleven frightened and discredited men in a back street in Jerusalem. It has now over one thousand million members throughout the world. *From the very earliest days growth has been of the essence of the Church.* This can only be explained by reference to the person, work and teaching of Jesus Christ, the Church's founder.

In the person of Christ men have discerned a life of compelling love, goodness, compassion, courage, sensitivity and grace; in the teaching of Christ men have discerned a quality of spiritual and moral insight unique in power and authority; in the resurrection of Christ men have discerned a saving work of God, demonstrating to all men for all time that goodness will triumph over evil, justice over injustice, hope over despair, love over hate, life over death. 'The theology of the future', wrote Professor John Macquarrie, 'will be a theology centred on God understood in terms of Jesus Christ.'[2]

From the earliest days Christians have affirmed that 'God was in Christ, reconciling the world unto himself', and have carried the good news of Christ to the ends of the earth. The impression created by Jesus Christ on his contemporaries finds expression in the pages of the New Testament and it is clear from these pages that the appeal of Jesus knew no limitations. 'I, if I be lifted up, will draw all men unto me.' 'Go ye therefore and teach all nations, baptizing them in the name of the Father, and of the Son and of the Holy Ghost: teaching them to observe all things whatsoever I have commanded you: and lo, I am with you always, even unto the end of the world.'

In recent years some New Testament scholars have questioned whether or not the words of 'The Great Commission' are the actual words of Jesus; what can never be questioned is the sheer historical fact of the missionary zeal of the early Church.

The Christian gospel focuses on the concept of 'The Kingdom of

God', a state of affairs in which men and women seek to do the will of God the Father by following the teaching and example of Christ the Son and in the power of the Holy Spirit. The parables of the Kingdom include parables of growth: the leaven spreading its transforming influence from within; the mustard seed growing up to the size of a great tree. The whole thrust of the teaching of Jesus was that of inner spiritual re-creation leading to the re-creation of society. 'Thy Kingdom come, thy will be done on earth as it is in heaven.'

To help to communicate his teaching about the Kingdom, Jesus selected and trained twelve disciples. The New Testament makes clear that when Jesus commissioned them to their task he instructed them to teach and to heal. 'And as ye go, preach, saying, The kingdom of heaven is at hand. Heal the sick, cleanse the lepers, raise the dead, cast out devils. . . .' (Matthew, 10. 7 and 8 AV). *From the very beginning, the communication of the faith and the ministry to human need were part of the one redemptive process.*

The theology of church growth cannot be elaborated in a short essay of this kind. What can be made clear is that it is rooted in the incarnation of Jesus Christ, in his proclamation of the Kingdom of God and in the ever-present reality of human need.

Some Principles of Church Growth

Research has shown that there is no one magic formula which will generate church growth under all circumstances.

'There is no single cause or simple pattern of causes related to church growth or decline. Rather, growth or decline involves a complex pattern of multiple and often interacting factors.'[3] Church growth is influenced by cultural and institutional factors at both national and local levels.

But research has also shown that there are certain basic principles which, when applied with faith, vigour and common sense by the institutional church, make for growth rather than for decline. The principles outlined very briefly below all interact; they are placed in numerical order only for reasons of clarity. How far these principles are currently applied throughout the Church of England as a whole, or in any particular church, is for the reader to decide.

1. Clear Beliefs, Strongly Held and Positively Affirmed

Ordinary decent English folk striving to make a living, pay their bills, bring up a family and lead a reasonably fulfilling life have neither time, talent, nor taste for academic theological speculation. They want to know what can reasonably be believed about God, about Jesus Christ and about the life after death, and they want to be convinced that these beliefs relate positively to the enhancement of their everyday lives. They expect the Church to be clear about its beliefs, and their expectation is entirely reasonable. When they find their expectations are unfulfilled they vote with their feet – and which way they have been voting in recent years is made all too clear by the statistics. In his contribution to a symposium of essays entitled *Great Christian Centuries to come* Professor John Macquarrie wrote, 'The decline of the Church in the 1960s was no doubt in part due to the common belief that the leaders of the Church no longer knew what they believed and were indeed abandoning the faith.'[4]

In his recent book, *Why Conservative Churches are Growing*,[5] a book widely *not* read in England, D. M. Kelley comments that fundamentalist and Pentecostal churches have increased their numbers at about the same proportional rate as the main line churches have decreased. The reason is straightforward: they are clear in their theological and moral convictions, positive in their affirmations and confident in their offer of salvation. Consider also the late Professor William Barclay who achieved enormous worldwide sales for his theological books and Bible commentaries – his 'Daily Study Bible' series sold over seven million copies in the English edition alone.[6] The reason is that, despite all his self-confessed limitations, he tried to communicate faith rather than doubt, conclusions rather than processes, clarity rather than confusion, and did so in terms which ordinary people could understand.

Not for one instant is it being implied that church growth calls for a retreat into dogmatic fundamentalism; it would be both dishonest and futile to pretend that the revolution in theology and

biblical studies which has taken place over the past hundred and
fifty years never happened. What matters is that clergy and lay
leaders have, and be seen to have, a positive and intelligent concern
for Christian truth, that they have thought and prayed their way
through to certain clear personal beliefs and are able to communicate their beliefs to ordinary people with conviction and
common sense.

It also matters that the Church as a whole should be seen to take
truth seriously, and that its official assemblies demonstrate at least
as much concern for doctrinal clarity as for social polemic, internal
reorganization or ecumenical dialogue.

2. The Wholeness of Growth

Church growth means growth in numbers, but it means much
more than that. There are other equally important dimensions of
growth, all of which interrelate.

Organic growth means the development of new structures within
the church to meet changing needs and circumstances. Examples of
this in England would be the rapid growth of the non-stipendiary
ministry and the development of group ministries serving the
needs of many small churches in rural areas.

Incarnational growth means the growing influence of Christian men
and women in the life and structures of society. Obvious examples
of this would be the involvement of Christian people in the work
of the Samaritans and of local race relations committees.

Spiritual growth means growth of church members in Christian
maturity, growth in prayer, knowledge and understanding,
growth in Christian fellowship and quality of life. This would
include Sunday schools, retreats, adult Christian education,
marriage enrichment courses, etc.

A growing church is growing in all these areas, not just in
numbers alone – quantity and quality nourish each other.

3. Desire for Growth

Many churches do not grow because they do not want to grow;
they are comfortable as they are. In most parishes of the Church of
England the assumption is that there are the 'faithful few' who will
support the church regularly, there are those 'on the fringe' who
appear at Christmas and Easter, but that most of the community
are 'not interested' except in so far as they wish to make use of the
church for baptisms, weddings and funerals. At best, the Church of
England is committed to a maintenance ministry – just trying to
keep going – and in many areas it is increasingly hard pressed even
to do that.

The desire for growth arises out of the conviction that if the
Christian faith is true then it is true *for all*, that membership of the
Church matters and that those outside the Church are missing
something which will enhance their lives. It is a conviction which
arises out of a high theology of the Church as the Body of Christ,
the living agent of God's saving purpose for individual people and
for mankind as a whole.

It needs to be affirmed that a church which is well led and well
organized bestows many precious benefits on its members:

a reasonable faith which gives meaning, purpose and value to life here
and hope for life hereafter.

personal values and ideals tested in the experience of centuries.

a ministry of worship, prayer, sacrament and spiritual teaching.

a ministry of pastoral care, particularly associated with the most deeply
significant of human experiences: birth, marriage, and death.

strength and inspiration for the constant demands of daily living.

opportunities for fellowship, service and spiritual growth.

opportunities for children and young people to grow up in an atmosphere of love and acceptance and to acquire worthwhile personal
standards and ideals.

There are millions who find their membership of the Church to be
not only important in itself but also to be *useful and creative*, a
positive influence making wholly for good in their own lives, the

lives of their families and in the life of the community. There are also very many who see the growth in numbers and influence of the world-wide Church as essential for mankind's ultimate survival, for man's greatest threat is his own inner spiritual disorder.

Out of convictions such as these comes the desire for growth; and one of the certain principles of the church growth movement is that no church will ever grow unless it wants to.

4. Planning for Growth

If desire is to be translated into achievement there must be research, thought, prayer and planning. In a church or cathedral which is committed to growth clergy and lay leaders need to study the neighbourhood and its needs; the composition, interests and talents of the congregation. In the light of this information they can then establish clear, challenging, faith-stretching goals for growth. Without such goals there can be no intelligent planning and without planning there can be no priorities. One of the most outstandingly successful practitioners of church growth, Dr Robert Schuller, has emphasized that 'a church which has no plans for growth has plans for no growth'. And it needs to be emphasized that planning must relate to every aspect of growth, incarnational, organic and spiritual, as well as numerical. Planning for growth does not imply an assertion of arrogant triumphalism.

5. Positive and Effective Leadership

This point may well provoke alarm as it conflicts with the cherished Anglican self-image of the devout and scholarly pastor quietly devoting himself to 'faithful parish work' and regarding considerations of growth and 'success' as unworthy and irrelevant.

But the fact must be faced that church growth research stresses again and again the vital importance of the quality of positive leadership shown by denominational leaders and parish clergy. In England the issue is complicated by the fact that the Church of England has been for centuries the 'Established Church' of the land and this constitutional arrangement is by no means dead. Bishops and clergy have responsibilities not only to the Church and its members but also more widely to the community. Deciding priorities of leadership in this context can be genuinely difficult and frustrating.

Many different qualities are required of a Christian minister, but the specific qualities relating to church growth are, in order of importance:

(a) Strong Christian motivation arising out of sincere belief and an active spiritual life of prayer, worship and study, including Bible study.

(b) Sincere conviction that membership of the Church matters and serves to enhance people's lives.

(c) Positive and enthusiastic attitudes, willingness to work and an absence of cynicism. Rare qualities in the clergy of a church which has been in decline for decades, where morale is low and which has had an obsessive concern for negative self-criticism.

(d) Clear personal aims and well-established priorities. There is a price to be paid for church growth and so far as the clergy are concerned it demands a rigorous concentration on essential tasks and a refusal to stray off down attractive by-ways. A parish clergyman who spends much of his time working as a counsellor with the local Marriage Guidance Council is no doubt making a useful contribution to society. But working for the Marriage Guidance Council is, quite simply, not what he is ordained and paid to do.

(e) The ability to inspire, motivate, instruct and organize others, particularly lay leaders. A growing church can never be a one-man band. A growing church is a church of the laity and the enabling of lay leadership is now one of the principal functions of the ordained ministry.

(f) Stability and perseverance – the willingness to stay put in appointments for a reasonable number of years. Men who move from job to job every three to five years achieve little because they do not stay long enough to see big plans through to a conclusion.

(g) Academic attainment. This point should not be misunderstood. No attempt is being made to deny the importance of an educated and intelligent ministry – it has never been more important in the whole of the Church's history. The point is that the specifically *academic* attainment of a clergyman is not, of itself, a significant factor in the growth of his church. Academic attainment needs to be complemented by the more basic qualities of conviction, common sense and kindness and by skills in communication.

6. Well Organized Churches

Growing churches in Europe and North America have certain easily recognizable features. They include:

(a) A ministry of welcome whereby persons coming to church are welcomed in a friendly way by other lay persons and put at their ease. Realistic and sympathetic provision will be made for their practical needs, such as sufficient parking space and crêche facilities for parents with young children. Failure to provide regular crêche facilities for young parents is tantamount to locking the church door in their face.

(b) An effective system whereby persons coming to church for the first time are recognized, welcomed and given every opportunity for incorporation into the church's membership. By 'effective system' is not meant one clergyman doing his best to be genial. The assimilation of new members is a process involving the specific training of lay persons, the taking and processing of records and the organization of follow up. Except in the very smallest of congregations it cannot be, and ought not to be, the duty of the clergy alone.

(c) Effective advertising and clearly visible notices so that members, visitors and unchurched persons are *very easily* able to discover the place and time of services and other church activities.

(d) Inspiring Sunday worship in appropriate surroundings with good music and opportunity for congregational participation.

(e) Positive preaching which communicates faith, hope, love and encouragement rather than doubt, gloom, controversy, fatuity, depression and boredom. Despite the best efforts of the College of Preachers in organizing training courses, the importance of preaching remains widely undervalued.

(f) An effective programme of Christian education for children, timed to coincide with the main Sunday service for adults. The importance of this cannot be overestimated. Church growth research makes clear that one of the most important factors in drawing young married adults to church is a well-organized Sunday School. The development of church-based programmes of Christian education is one of the most obviously urgent of the Church's priorities. Not only does the Sunday School provide Christian nurture for the children of church members, it is also a highly effective means of outreach to unchurched families.

(g) An effective programme of adult Christian education offering courses relating to the needs and interests of persons of all ages, and involving work in small groups. These courses will provide basic learning in the areas of Bible study, doctrine, prayer and Christian living, but they will also include courses which prepare lay persons for their specific ministerial tasks, e.g., as teachers, counsellors, lay pastors, hospital visitors, etc.

(h) An effectively organized system of pastoral care. It is impossible for one or two clergymen, by themselves, to exercise responsible pastoral care over hundreds of church members and possibly thousands of parishioners. This can only be achieved through the formation of many local neighbourhood groups with eight to ten families in each group. The pastoral care of the members of each group will be the responsibility of a trained lay person. The clergy will be informed of persons in special need, but their primary function will be the training and care of the lay ministers. Effective pastoral care in the twentieth century will increasingly depend on lay people learning to care for other lay people.

(j) An effective ministry in the area of *Marriage and Family Life*.

This will include:

careful preparation of those about to be married. If the Church is to continue to proclaim a high ideal of marriage then it is essential that persons receive competent preparation. How else can they hope to attain the ideal presented to them?

marriage enrichment courses for the married. Marriage encounter and marriage enrichment courses have grown in popularity in recent years. The purpose of these courses is to enable the happily married to stay happily married — an increasing need when men and women are marrying younger, living longer and when the institution of marriage is subject to many conflicting pressures.

a special ministry to single persons. In some areas *one person in three* is single: either unmarried, separated, divorced or widowed. Such persons have special needs and a ministry specifically for them is an essential pastoral provision.

(k) A very wide range of fellowship groups to meet the social needs of persons of all kinds. It is not sufficient that opportunity be provided for the congregation to meet and talk over coffee for half an hour after the Sunday service, desirable though this is. It is also important that each person belongs to some smaller group in which he or she is known, accepted, loved and valued as a person.

It will by now be sufficiently obvious that a well-organized church cannot possibly be run by the clergy alone; an essential contribution is the extensive use of trained lay persons. The average congregation contains men and women with a wide range of spiritual gifts and talents; one of the most vital functions of the clergy is to enable these persons to recognize and use their gifts in the service of the church. Full recognition of the importance of the ministry of the laity is one of the cardinal principles of church growth.

7. A Positive Approach to Finance

There are some in the Church who view money matters with suspicion and dislike; they regard discussion about finance and fund-raising as somehow unspiritual and demeaning. The fact is that money is a commodity like any other. As paper is needed for Bible, stone for walls, lead for roofs, glass for windows and wood for doors, so we need money. It is a commodity which, with others, makes possible the Church's ministry. Britain is a nation of vast, staggering wealth – consider only the astronomical sums spent annually on alcohol, tobacco and gambling. In his book *Your Church has real Possibilities*, Dr Robert Schuller emphasizes the huge amount of wealth in the world and asserts that 'No church has a money problem. It is always a symptom not a problem. The real problem is a lack of dynamic, need-filling ideas, a lack of energy, vision, nerve or faith.'[7] There is no shame in raising money for a great cause, and there is no greater cause than that of Christ and his Church. It is a very great evil that churches should be hindered in any way by financial stringency. A well-managed financial development programme using the best available methods of stewardship and fund-raising is a feature of all growing churches.

There is one important word of warning. The strength of any religious denomination lies in its local congregations and this demands that growth in income be made available for the needs of local churches. So far as the Church of England is concerned, this means that quota payments imposed on parishes need to be kept under most critical scrutiny. A denomination which demands increasingly heavy quota payments from local churches to support central bodies, however worthy they may be thought to be, is hacking at its own roots.

8. Operational Research

One of the characteristics of the church growth movement is what has been described as *consecrated empiricism*: a readiness to use pastoral techniques which are found to be effective and an equal readiness to discard those which are not. Essential to this is constant research and experiment at every level and in all areas of the Church's work and behind this is the key question: 'How can we do better?'

For the local church this would include:

(a) Careful study of the make-up of the local community; awareness of changes within the community; the nature of the main social and occupational groups; particular needs of the community and how far they are met by existing agencies; particular needs that could be met by the church, etc.

(b) Careful study of the membership of the congregation; predominant age groups; trends in membership; particular needs of church members; geographical distribution of members, etc.

This type of information is essential for planning and the setting of realistic goals.

There must also be a central agency which can co-ordinate research as a whole and publish the more significant findings. This might include: examples of significant numerical growth in urban churches; examples of effective new developments in Christian education; instances of significant growth in other churches elsewhere in the world.

No well-managed business, industrial company or political party could continue without a department entirely devoted to research and development. The need for this in the Church is all too apparent.

Some Criticisms of Church Growth

It is no surprise to find that the church growth movement has its critics. Some of the more serious objections have been:

(a) That it is largely concerned with growth in numbers.

Study of much of the existing church growth literature makes clear that this criticism is valid. But it should be recognized that the church growth movement is of relatively recent origin; emphasis on numerical growth can be justified by the fact that this is, at present, the area of greatest need.

(b) That it is hostile to ecumenism.

If this was true it would be a serious objection. Dr F. W. Dillistone in his essay 'On looking back' has rightly emphasized that growth in understanding and co-operation between the churches has been one of the most valued developments in the world-wide Church in this century. The issue is simply one of priorities. Advocates of church growth ask the question: Which is the more urgently important?

to communicate the Christian faith to unchurched people, disciple them into the Church's fellowship and ensure their pastoral care, or to engage in lengthy and detailed discussions with other Christians about matters of ecclesiastical organization and differences of belief?

And to reply that both are important is to evade the issue, particularly in England where the vast majority of the population have no effective contact with the Church and view denominational disputes with weariness and incredulity. Nor is it possible to argue that ecumenical co-operation stimulates church growth: there is no significant evidence to suggest that this is so.

(c) That it denies equality of status to all world religions.

This criticism contains a measure of truth. Advocates of church growth do not subscribe to the view that all the religions of the world are equally true, equally false and equally useless; they do not accept that there is some lowest common denominator in all religions which will eventually emerge as mankind's creed. While respecting the beliefs of others, recognizing the need for dialogue with them, and accepting that there are many ways of revelation, they nevertheless proclaim the uniqueness of God's revelation in Jesus Christ, 'the Light which lighteth every man that cometh into the world' (John 1. 9 AV), and maintain that the Church's task is faithfulness to that revelation. If there is to be creative dialogue between the world's great religions it will not come about through a confused comprehensiveness.

(d) That it is inadequately concerned for social and political issues.

It is true that advocates of church growth are not exponents of any particular 'political theology'. But it is no less true that an essential dimension of church growth is 'incarnational growth', which includes Christian men and women bringing their insights and principles to every aspect of social and political life. The policy is one of redemption through involvement in the existing agencies of society rather than clergy-directed social activism. The primary function of clergy and ministers is seen as ministering to the gathered congregation – enabling the laity for their work of Christian service and influence.

(e) That it is unrealistic and creates expectations which cannot everywhere be fulfilled, so aggravating guilt and frustration among clergy and lay leaders who feel to have 'failed'.

Of all criticisms this is the most mistaken. Advocates of church growth constantly stress the need for consecrated empiricism. If a church is in decline, then thought and research are needed to examine the reasons for decline – it may be in an area where growth has become impossible. In his book *Your Church can be Healthy*,[8] Dr Peter Wagner lists a variety of ecclesiastical 'diseases' and recognizes that certain of them are terminal: e.g. an old-established church in an inner-city location whose catchment area has totally changed through an influx of Moslem immigrants. Church growth combines strong faith, devotion to the church and concern for human need, with common sense, realism and respect for pastoral experience.

Cathedrals and Growth

The essay by the Dean of St Paul's (chapter 4) shows that the ancient cathedrals are now more used than ever before in history; they have long since ceased to be the 'retreats of learned leisure' portrayed in the novels of Anthony Trollope. Jumbo jets, coaches and cars bring visitors by the million from all over the world. The result of this is a growing pressure upon many cathedrals – not least for financial reasons – to consider themselves as part of the tourist industry and it is a pressure which needs to be resisted.

Cathedrals were built as great churches, not as ecclesiastical tourist centres and it is as great churches serving the needs of visitors, diocese and congregations that they must develop during the next decade. Not only are the principles of church growth relevant to the future of the cathedral ministry, but cathedrals themselves should become centres of study and development in this area. The foreseeable objection that the ancient cathedrals are not parish churches has long since been overtaken by events – a fact which needs to be accepted rather than deplored.

Conclusion

What has been written in this short article presents no more than a brief and inadequate introduction to some of the principles of church growth as they relate to the Church of England in the 1980s. Most will have concluded by now that there is nothing much that is new; and that is quite correct.

One of the leading exponents of church growth in the U.S.A., Dr Peter Wagner, has commented that it is very common for a person who has completed a training seminar in church growth to say 'Everything I heard I have known before. But this is the first time it has all come together in a useful way.'[9]

Dr Donald McGavran, addressing an Advanced Church Growth seminar in Pasadena in April 1980, described the principles of church growth as 'sanctified common sense'. It is precisely for this reason that they are important for the Church of England at this time. Church growth is not a campaign, a crusade, or a stunt. Church leaders in England are cautious about such activities and well they might be in the light of experience since 1945. It is also worth noting that a recent research project in the U.S.A. recorded that 0·001% of church members came to join their church as a result of 'evangelistic crusade'. Church growth is not a temporary fizzle, it is a whole new way of life for the whole church.

What is the alternative? In the absence of any other credible initiative it is, quite simply, continuing decline. But the decline will not be uniform; Evangelicals and Anglo-Catholics will, because of their commitment and enthusiasm, draw more people into their respective camps. England will experience even more seriously what Professor Martin Marty has described as the 'collapse of the centre', both in theological thought and religious institutions. Yet 'It so often seems that a God who cares about the world would bless churches that care for wholeness and civility and not merely for aggressive pouncing on prospects as possible converts.'[10]

The Church of England has a long and distinguished tradition of theological scholarship, literary achievement, spirituality, missionary endeavour, educational initiative, social concern, and, above all, worship and pastoral care. That a church so concerned for 'wholeness and civility' should finally wither into an insignificant sect will neither glorify God nor serve the needs of man.

The renewal of the Church will not be achieved by indirect influences, however important they may be. It is true that millions watch religious programmes on TV and it is true that many of these programmes are of superior quality to much that can be seen on Sunday TV in North America. But watching religious programmes on TV is for most a spectator activity, requiring no commitment and providing neither consistent teaching, personal fellowship nor pastoral care.

Twenty years ago there were many who stressed the importance of Christian education, pointing out that whereas only a small proportion of children were in contact with the Church, all received religious teaching at day school. The provision of religious instruction was a legal obligation under the terms of the 1944 Education Act and much of the instruction provided was firmly based on the Bible. Church and school were seen as partners in the task of the nation's spiritual renewal.

All that has largely passed away. Developments in religious education in recent years have been such that the concept of 'Christian education' in county schools has been formally abandoned. Many newly-revised syllabuses make clear that religious education in schools is now *teaching about religions*, including Christianity; the aim is educational, not evangelistic

The renewal of the institutional Church is unlikely to come about through the TV tube or the classroom – that is not the purpose of either religious broadcasting or religious education. It will, under God, come about through faithful and intelligent application of the principles of church growth. In his fine book *Leaders of the Church of England 1828–1978*, David Edwards wrote 'it has become clear that the Church of England is to be led, if it is to be led at all, by people influencing other people in groups.'[11] That is how the church growth movement will develop in England in the years which lie ahead. It is likely that there will be three main stages:

(a) the initial training of selected clergy and lay leaders by existing trained consultants.

(b) the further training of some of the best of these men and women as *church growth consultants*.

Some of these persons will wish to obtain further qualifications and experience by attending accredited training institutions in the U.S.A. Every diocese will eventually have several church growth consultants. Most of these will be active clergy with parish or cathedral appointments; they will certainly not be 'advisers' removed from pastoral duty, housed in a central office and paid by central funds. The main function of church growth consultants is to initiate growth programmes at parish level, a task involving careful preparation, effective presentation and a lengthy period of after-care.

(c) the setting up of a central agency responsible for the co-ordination of research, publications, training and forward planning.

During the next twenty years the Church of England will experience steady growth and renewal. In the year 2000 we shall look back with astonishment at the confusion, negativism and gloom which characterized the 1960s and 70s. Growth is of the essence of the Church because the Church is the Church of Jesus Christ, whom God raised from the dead to demonstrate to all men for all time that good will triumph over evil, hope over despair, love over hate and life over death.

NOTES

1. 'Church going', *The Less Deceived*. Marvell Press.
2. *Great Christian Centuries to Come* (Mowbrays 1974), p. 167.
3. Hoge and Roozen, *Understanding Church Growth and Decline* (Pilgrim Press 1979), p. 39.
4 Op. cit., p. 162.
5. Harper & Row 1977.

6. R. D. Kernohan, *William Barclay* (Hodder 1980), p. 51.
7. Regal Books 1974, p. 158.
8. Abingdon Press 1979.
9. Hoge and Roozen, op. cit., p. 271.
10. Hoge and Roozen, op. cit., p. 14.
11. Hodder & Stoughton 1978, p. 367.

Postscript

The Very Reverend MICHAEL STANCLIFFE
Dean of Winchester

Common but careless thinking suggests to many people today that growth means the process of getting bigger and bigger, with the further suggestion that getting bigger and bigger means getting better and better. But the foregoing pages will have been misunderstood if a reader supposes that this is what growth means to those who have written them. The contributors to *Grow or Die* are not unmindful of such other books as *Small is Beautiful* or *Enough is Enough* – or, for that matter, *The Gospel according to St Mark*, *The Acts of the Apostles* and the *Epistle to the Ephesians*.

If we make the mistake of thinking of it solely in terms of magnitude or improvement, it is because the word growth, meaning originally the organic development of the living body of a plant or animal, has for long been used figuratively and commonly of all manner of other forms of development. We see the sky grow cloudy, feel the weather grow colder, sense the sea growing rougher. We can observe the growth of things as various as a block of flats, a work of art, a bank balance, a newspaper's circulation, a party's power or a person's understanding, efficiency or influence. We speak of the growth of reputations, suspicions, hopes, fears, and we can chart on a graph the growth of a country's population or the number of its crematoria. But in all such examples growth means something rather different from what it means to a mother watching the development of her child, or to that child, now grown up, watching the mother grow old.

Nor is such a figurative use of the word of recent origin. The New Testament writers speak of the growth of the gospel, of knowledge, of unrighteousness; and indeed it is to be recognized that St Luke was not shy of counting heads when describing the growth of the word of God and how the churches increased in number daily.

But in all such New Testament uses the original sense of growth as organic development is not far below the surface. The Church's first writers were much nearer the natural processes of growth than are most of us, and when they wrote of anything increasing it was from the standpoint of, and out of the experience of, men who were familiar in a way that we are not with the lilies of the field and how they grow; with seed growing secretly, they knew not how; with fields growing white unto harvest; with tares, that they also grow; with grass growing on the housetop which withers before it is plucked up; with a boy growing in wisdom and stature, and in favour with God and man. The Christians at Ephesus were told that they were members of a structure which 'is joined together and grows into a holy temple in the Lord, in whom you also are built into it for a dwelling place of God'; but only just behind the building metaphor here lies the natural image of the Church as a body of which Christ is the head 'from which the whole body grows with a growth that is from God'.

Passing reference should also be made to another form of natural growth which is quite distinct from the development of a living organism and which probably lies behind the record of the Fourth Gospel that John the Baptist said of Jesus that 'He must increase, but I must decrease'. There are those who interpret this as meaning that Jesus would attract a growing number of adherents while the number following the Baptist would diminish. But the probability appears to be that John was not comparing the size of two bodies but the strength of two lights, the natural image being that of the dawn with its gradual increase of radiance streaming from the sun and before which the morning stars pale into invisibility.

Be that as it may, it remains true that, in the great majority of cases, growth in the New Testament – and not least in the parables of Jesus – is understood in terms of the development of a living body, generally a plant, and no consideration of the growth of the

Church in our own day will be fully appreciated without some sensitivity to that fact and some awareness of its echoes.

So growth is the gift of God and part of his creative activity. Man can help – or hinder – the process, in so far as he sees to it, or fails to see to it, that the ground is properly prepared, cleared of weeds and stones, the seed sown, the young plants not trampled on, the crows scared off. But there is little else he can do; the earth produces of itself, first the blade, then the ear, then the full corn in the ear while the husbandman sleeps and rises night and day for a period of months. The human contribution is certainly not unimportant; such as it is it is essential, and we are fellow labourers with God. But though Paul plants and Apollos waters it is God that gives the increase.

And such husbandry calls for much patience and a proper sense of values. The process of growth is slow when measured in minutes hours and days; it cannot be discerned by the human eye, and it can be slowed down, even set back, by climatic conditions over which man has little control. There is little in the New Testament or in the subsequent history of the Church to encourage the use of glass-house techniques to force the development of the Kingdom of God. Nor are we to be misled into thinking that the biggest seed or the most obvious shoot is necessarily that which will count for most when the harvest comes. The growth-points that are really significant may be very small or even hidden altogether.

Above all, the New Testament compels us to recognize that growth is inevitably a process of change, and not so much a continuous change for 'the better' but a development towards a point, a climax, the bearing of fruit – after which there is what looks like a change for 'the worse', for the plant may be said to have done its work for the year, or for ever if it be an annual. The grass withers, the flower falls, and only the Word of the Lord continues for ever. The seed falls to earth and is buried. Unless it die it abides by itself alone. But if it dies it bears much fruit. The Church in its *earthly forms and historical structures* is subject to the same laws as all living matter. 'Grow or die' has to be matched with 'Grow *and* die', even paradoxically with 'Die to grow'. But a Church which has at the heart of its faith the death and the resurrection of its Lord Jesus Christ will not be afraid to accept the consequences of that paradox, and will grow more alive through its acceptance, knowing that it is God who gives the increase and that the brightest morning stars grow pale in the light of the New Creation.

Notes on the Authors

The Reverend Canon Frederick Dillistone, D.D.

Ordained in Winchester Cathedral 1927; Curate of St Jude's, Southsea 1927–9; Tutor Wycliffe Hall, Oxford 1929–31; Missionary in N. India 1931–2; Curate of St James', Alperton 1932–4; Vicar of St Andrew's, Oxford 1934–8; Professor of Systematic Theology, Wycliffe College, Toronto 1938–45; Vice-Principal, London College of Divinity 1945–7; Professor of Theology, Episcopal Theological School, Cambridge, Mass., 1947–52; Canon Residentiary of Liverpool Cathedral 1952–6; Dean of Liverpool 1956–63; Fellow and Chaplain, Oriel College, Oxford, 1964–70.

The Very Reverend John R. Gray, D.D.

Assistant Minister, The Barony Church, Glasgow 1939–41; Chaplain, Royal Navy 1941–6; Minister, St Stephen's Parish Church, Glasgow, 1946–66; Minister of Dunblane Cathedral since 1966.
Moderator of the General Assembly of the Church of Scotland 1977.

The Right Reverend Colin James, M.A.

Curate of St Dunstan's, Stepney, London, 1952–5; Chaplain of Stowe School, 1955–9; Producer, Religious Broadcasting Department of B.B.C. 1959–67; Vicar of Bournemouth 1967–73; Canon Residentiary of Winchester Cathedral and Bishop Suffragan of Basingstoke 1973–7; Bishop of Wakefield since 1977.

The Reverend Canon James Robertson, M.A.

Curate in Edinburgh 1940–5; Missionary in Northern Rhodesia
1945–50; Warden, St Mark's Training College Mapanza 1950–5;
Chalimbana Training College, Zambia 1955–65; Lecturer, Bede
College, Durham 1965–8; Secretary of Council of Church
Colleges of Education 1968–73; General Secretary of The United
Society for the Propagation of the Gospel since 1973.

The Very Reverend Michael Stancliffe, M.A.

Curate of St James, Southbroom 1940–3; Curate of Ramsbury
1943–4; Curate of Cirencester 1944–9; Chaplain, Westminster
School, 1949–57; Preacher at Lincoln's Inn, 1954–7; Canon of
Westminster Abbey and Rector of St Margaret's Church, West-
minster, 1957–69; Chaplain to the Speaker of the House of
Commons 1961–9; Dean of Winchester since 1969.

The Right Reverend John V. Taylor, D.D.

Curate of All Souls, Langham Place, London 1938–40; Curate of
St Helens, Lancashire, 1940–3; C.M.S. Missionary in Uganda
1945–55; Member, International Missionary Council 1955–9;
Africa Secretary of Church Missionary Society 1959–63; General
Secretary of C.M.S. 1963–74; Bishop of Winchester since 1975.

The Very Reverend Alan Webster, M.A., B.D.

Curate of Attercliffe, Sheffield 1942–4; Curate of Arbourthorne
1944–6; Chaplain of Westcott House, Cambridge 1946–8; Vice-
Principal 1948–53; Vicar of Barnard Castle 1953–9; Warden of
Lincoln Theological College 1959–70; Dean of Norwich 1970–77;
Dean of St Paul's since 1977.

The Reverend Canon Alexander Wedderspoon, M.A., B.D.

Curate of Kingston Parish Church 1961–3; Lecturer in Religious Education, University of London 1963–6; Education Adviser to Church of England Schools Council and Secretary to the Commission on Religious Education 1966–9; Assistant Priest St Margaret's Church, Westminster 1967–70; Canon Residentiary of Winchester Cathedral since 1970.